Roots, Suffixes, Prefixes

1st Edition

B.A. REED

AuthorHouse™
1663 Liberty Drive, Suite 200
Bloomington, IN 47403
www.authorhouse.com
Phone: 1-800-839-8640

First published by AuthorHouse 5/21/2009

ISBN: 978-1-4389-6670-0 (sc)

Library of Congress Control Number: 2009902490

Printed in the United States of America
Bloomington, Indiana

This book is printed on acid-free paper.

PREFACE

Medical Roots, Suffixes and Prefixes is a new member of American Commercial College. It is a resource guide for students in the Allied Health field. It is a guide that can be used easily in the classroom as a tool for students who are introduced to medical terms. It will serve as an aide to students who are having difficulty in dividing words. Students will learn the origin of words in their root and began to string them as they understand the basic suffixes and prefixes that apply.

It is hoped that this book provides the convenience for students in the study of the medical language as they note the division of words into their component parts: roots, prefixes, suffixes. This book is a useful tool for the medical student (nurses, medical assistants, nurse assistants, etc.) who is learning a language where these components provide a base for the meaning of these terms. Because of the many roots, prefixes, suffixes in use – there may be many not included. If you should find one excluded, we appreciate you writing us for our next edition. We welcome any comments or corrections.

Please write:

American Commercial College
B.A. Reed
3177 Executive Drive
San Angelo, Texas 76901

ROOTS - SUFFIXES - PREFIXES

The major components of medical terminology are: Roots, prefixes and suffixes.

Root Words:
The root word provides the basic meaning of the word. It is the basic lexical. It provides its nature and meaning. The root word in medical terminology is combined with another root, prefix or suffix. There is separation of the combining forms by an "o" or "i". The root carries significant aspects of semantic content as defined in <u>Wikipedia, The Free</u> <u>Encyclopedia.</u>

Prefixes:
The term prefix means to put or attach in front of. It is an affix attached in front of a word. It produces a derivative word with a new meaning. Prefixes are commonly used to help describe the appearance of, or location of an anatomical part.

Suffix: (postfix, ending)
A suffix is an affix added to the end of a word or stem serving to form a new. It can be placed after a root. It also changes the word's meaning as well as its function (use).

Suffixes most commonly used in the medical science to indicate disease are "itis" meaning inflammation; "oma" meaning tumors; and "osis" meaning condition, usually abnormal condition.

Your knowledge of these word elements and how they are combined to form common medical terms will make the most complicated medical terminology decipherable.

CONTENTS

a–	lack, not, away from, outside of, no, without.
ab–	away from (notice the b faces away from the a).
abdomen–	abdomen.
abdomin–	abdomen, abdominal.
abio–	nonliving, nonviable.
–ac	pertaining to, similar to.
acanth–	thorn, thorny, spine, spiny.
acantho–	thorn, thorny, spine, spiny.
acar–	mite, itch.
acari–	mite, itch.
acaro–	"pertaining to mites".
acaro–	mite, itch.
–aceae	a suffix used in combination with the name of one of the principal general to from the names of families of plants and bacteria.
–aceous	of the nature of something specified.
–aceous	pertaining to or characterized by.
acephalo–	having no head.
acet–	connection with or derived from acetic acid or acetyl.

A

acetabul-	acetabulum (hip socket).
aceto-	connection with or derived from.
-acid	acid.
acid-	sour, acid.
-acidemia	increased hydrogen-.
acous	hearing.
-acousia	(specified) condition of hearing.
-acoustic	pertaining to the hearing organs.
acr-	extremities, top, extreme point.
-acria	a condition of the extremities.
acro-	extremity, tip, end, height extreme, intense.
acryl-	acrylic.
acrylo-	acrylic.
act-	to do, drive, act.
actin-	ray, radiant; radiated structure.
actino-	ray, radiant; radiated structure.
acu-	needle; hearing (also see acou-).
acu-	sharp, severe, sudden.
-acusia	(specified) condition of hearing.
acuti-	acute, acutely angled.
acuto-	acute.

-ad	an adverbial suffix meaning –ward, toward.
ad-	toward (notice the d faces toward the a).
adelph-	sibling; twin, double, multiple; grouping of like units.
adelpho-	sibling; twin, double, multiple; grouping of like units.
-adelphus	inferior duplicity in conjoined twins.
aden-	gland, glandular.
-adenia	(condition of) the glands.
adeno-	gland, glandular.
adenoid-	adenoids.
adip-	fat (see lip- and steat-).
adip-	fat.
-adrenia	(degree or condition of) adrenal activity.
-aemia	blood condition.
-aemia	denoting (specified) condition of the blood or presence in the blood of a (specified) substance.
aer-	air, aerial; gas, gases.
aero	air.

A

-aesthesia   (condition of) feeling, perception, or sensation.

aesthesio-   sense, sensory, sensation.

-age   cumulative result; rate; action or process.

-agnosia   (condition of the) loss of the faculty to perceive.

-agog   a substance that induces or promotes secretion or expulsion.

-agog   an agent promoting the expulsion of a (specified) substance.

-agogue   an substance promoting the expulsion of a (specified) substance.

agon-   antagonistic muscles, which oppose each other.

-agon   assemble, gather together.

-agra   pain, painful seizure.

-al   characterized by combining for designating a compound containing a member of the aldehyde group.

alb-   white, whitish.

alb-   white; white corpus albicans of the ovary, a white scar tissue.

albino-	white.
albo-	white, whitish.
albumin-	albumin (a protein in the blood).
-albuminuria	(specified) condition characterized by excess serum proteins in urine.
ald-	aldehyde; relating to an aldehyde.
-ale	characterized by.
alg-	pain; pertaining to pain.
alge-	pain.
alges-	excessive.
algesi-	pain.
-algesia	(condition of) sensitivity to pain.
-algesic	pertaining to sensitivity to pain.
-algia	pain, painful condition.
-algic	related to pain.
algio-	pain; pertaining to pain.
algo-	pain; pertaining to pain.
ali-	wing; shaped like a wing, (as in certain organs or structures).
-alis	pertaining to something specified---alkaline alkal.
alkoxy-	(chemistry) a combining form denoting alkoxyl.

A

all-   other, different; variant, alternate, modified, others; deviant, abnormal.

allant-   allantioic, allantoid.

allelo-   another.

allelo-   reciprical; complimentany; alternate; alternative.

allo-   differing from the normal, reversal, or referring to another.

allotri-   abnormal, strange, unusual.

allotrio-   abnormal, strange, unusual.

allox-   a combining form denoting alloxan.

alve-   trough, channel, cavity.

alveoli-   alveolus, air sac.

ambi-   on both sides.

ambly-   obtuse, dull, faint.

ambo-   both.

ameb-   ameba, amebic, ameboid.

-ameba   (specified) protozoan--amoeba (specified) protozoan.

ammoni-   ammonium.

amni-	amnion (sac surrounding the embryo in the uterus.
amnio-	amnion.
amph-	on both sides.
amphi-	on both sides.
ampho-	both.
amyl-	starch.
amylo-	starch.
an-	anus.
-an	belonging to, characteristic of, similar to
an-	no, not without.
ana-	again, anew.
ana-	backward.
ana-	upward, excessive, again.
-anaemia	(condition of) red blood cell deficiency or its remedy.
anastomos-	a surgery connection.
anchylo-	bent, in the form of a loop.
ancylo-	bent, in the form of a loop.
andr-	man, male, masculine.
andro-	man, male, masculine.

A

-ane   a combining form designating hydrocarbons of the paraffin series.

-anemia   (condition of) red blood cell deficiency or its remedy.

anemo-   wind.

aneurysm   widening of a vessel.

angi-   vessel.

-angina   severe ulceration, usually of the mouth or throat.

angio-   vessel, vascular.

-angioma   tumor composed chiefly of blood and lymph vessels.

anhydr-   waterless, lacking fluid.

anis-   unequal.

aniso-   unequal or dissimilar.

ankyl-   stiff.

ankylo-   bent, in the form of a loop.

ano   anus, anal.

anomalo-   uneven, irregular.

-anopia   nonuse or arrested development of the eye.

-anopsia   nonuse or arrested development of the eye.

-ans	a combining form meaning "ing".
-ant	a suffix denoting an agent or thing that promotes a specific action.
ant-	against.
ante-	before, forward.
anter-	front.
anth-	a combining form denoting the presence of the anthracene nucleus.
antho-	a combining form denoting the presence of the anthracene nucleus.
anthraco-	a carbuncle.
anthrop-	human being, man.
anthropo-	man, human being.
anti-	against, opposed to; combating, preventing; alleviating; situated opposite.
antr-	an antrum or sinus.
antro-	an antrum or sinus.
ants	flower, floral, flower-like.
anxi	uneasy, anxious, distressed.
aort-	aorta, aortic.

A

ap-	away from, from; deprived, separated; derived from.
aph-	away from, from; deprived, separated; derived from.
-apheresis	removal, a carrying away.
-aphia	condition of the sense of touch.
-aphrodisia	(specified) condition of sexual arousal.
api-	bee.
apic-	apex, apical.
apici-	apex, apical.
apico-	apex, apical.
apio-	bee.
apo-	separation.
append-	appendix.
appendic-	appendix.
aque-	water.
-ar	pertaining to.
arachno-	arachnoid membrane.
arbor	a treelike pattern of white matter.
-arche	beginning.
archi-	first, beginning, original.
archo-	rectum or anus.

arter-	artery.
arteri-	artery.
arthr-	joint.
articul-	joint.
-ary	pertaining to.
-ase	enzyme.
-asthenia	lack of strength.
astro-	star, star-shaped.
-ate	acted upon or being in a (specified) state: a chemical compound derived from a (specified) source; an acid compound.
atelo-	imperfect or incomplete.
ather-	yellowish plaque, fatty substance.
atm-	(combining form) vapor; gas, air.
atom-	vapor; gas, air.
-atresia	combining form meaning closed or imperforate.
atret-	imperforate, imperforation.
atreto-	closed, imperforate.
atri-	atrium, upper heart chamber.

A

-atrophia	condition of malnutrition; 2. progressive decline of a body part.
-ature	a noun-forming combining form.
audi-	hearing; the sense of hearing.
audio-	auditory, hearing; sound.
audit-	hearing.
aur-	ear.
auri-	gold; in chemistry, the presence of gold in the trivalent or auric state.
auricul-	ear.
auriculo-	auricle, auricular.
auro-	ear.
auro-	gold; in chemistry, the presence of gold in the univalent or aurous state.
auscult	listen.
aut-	self, one's own, spontaneous, independent.
auto-	self, one's own, spontaneous, independent.
automat-	automatic, spontaneous, initiatory.
-auxe	denoting hypertrophy, enlargement.

auxo-	denoting growth; increase; in biochemistry, accelerating or stimulating.
auxo-	growth, acceleration, stimulation.
ax-	axis.
ax-	denoting axon; axis cylinder.
axi-	axis, axial.
axill-	armpit.
axio-	axis.
axo-	denoting axon; axis cylinder.
axono-	axis; axon.
az-	indicates the presence of nitrogen or of the group -n:n- within a compound.
azi-	the presence of a group.
azo-	indicates the presence of nitrogen or of the group –n:n- within a compound.
azot-	nitrogen, nitrogenous.
azota-	(combining form) nitrogen, nitrogenous.

B

bacill-   bacillus.

bacill-   rod-shaped bacterium.

bacilli-   (combining form) bacillus.

bacillo-   (combining form) bacillus.

bacter-   any bacterial microorganism.

-bacter   denoting a bacterial organism.

bacteri-   bacteria.

-bacteria   genus of microscopic plants forming the class schizomycetes.

bacterio-   any bacterial microorganism.

balan-   glans penis.

balano-   glans penis.

ballisto-   missiles, projectiles.

bar-   denoting weight, pressure; atmospheric pressure.

-barbituric   an acid used medicinally for its soporific effects.

baro-   weight, pressure; atmospheric pressure.

bary-   heavy or difficult.

bas-   base (alkaline, the   opposite of acid).

basal   base.

basi-	1. base; lower part. 2. Chemical base.
-basia	ability to walk.
-basic	relating or containing alkaline compounds.
basilo-	base, basilar.
basio-	pertaining to a foundation or a base.
baso-	base, basic; basal.
bath-	depth; downward, under.
batho-	depth; downward, under.
bathy-	deep, low.
bi-	life.
bi-	life; pertaining to living organisms.
bio-	life.
bi-	denoting two, twice, double; anatomy: connection with or relation to each of two symmetrically paired parts; chemistry: presence of two atoms.
-bia	creature possessing a mode of life.
biblio-	(combining form) book.
bil-	gall, bile.

B

bili-	bile, biliary; derived from bile.
bilirubin-	biliburin (bile pigment).
bin-	two, two at a time.
bio-	life.
-biosis	life.
-biotic	pertaining to life.
bis-	twice, both; chemistry: the doubling of a complex expression.
-blast	denoting a sprout, shoot, germ: biology: a formative cell, germ layer.
-blastema	mass of living substance.
-blastic	germinating, arising, growing.
-blastoma	immature tumor.
-blastula	an early embryonic stage in development of a fertilized egg.
blenn-	mucus.
blenno-	mucus.
blephar-	eyelid.
-blepharia	condition of the eyelid.
-blepsia	condition of sight.
-blepsy	condition of sight.
bol-	to cast (throw).

bor-	boron.
boro-	boron.
bothri-	bothrium.
bothrio-	bothrium.
-boulia	condition of the will.
brachi	arm.
brachi-	arm; brachial.
-brachia	an anatomical condition involving an arm.
brachio-	arm; brachial.
-brachium	arm or armlike growth.
brachy-	short (distance).
brady-	slow.
branchi-	gill; branchial.
brepho-	embryo, fetus, newborn infant.
brevi-	short.
brom-	odor, stench.
bromo-	odor, stench.
bronc-	bronchial tubes (two tubes, one right and one left, that branch from the trachea to enter the lungs).
bronch-	bronchial tube.
bronch-	bronchus.

B

bronchi-   bronchus.

bronchiol-   bronchiole, small bronchus.

bry-   full of life.

bucc-   cheek.

bucca-   cheek.

bucci-   cheek.

bucco-   cheek.

bulbo-   bulb, bulbar.

-bulia   (condition of the) will.

-bund   prone to something specified.

burs-   bursa.

but-   a substance or compound containing a group of four carbon atoms.

buto-   a substance or compound containing a group of four carbon atoms.

butyr-   butter.

butyr-   butyric.

butyro-   butyric.

C

cac-	bad, diseased, deformed.
-cace	denotes a bad, diseased, or deformed condition.
caco-	bad, diseases, deformed.
-caine	(a combining form) denotes an anesthetic compound or substance.
-caine	a combining form naming synthetic alkaloid anesthetics.
calc-	(combining form) denoting calcium; calcium salts.
calc-	lime, limestone.
calcane-	calcaneus (heel).
calcaneo-	(combining form) denoting calcaneus, calcaneal.
calci-	(combining form) denoting calcium; calcium salts.
calci-	calcium.
calco-	(combining form) denoting calcium; calcium salts.
cali-	calyx (calyx).
calor-	calories.
calor-	heat.
cancr-	cancer.

C

canth-   (a combining form) denoting canthus, canthal.

cantho-   (a combining form) denoting canthus, canthal.

capill   capillaries.

capit-   head.

capn-   carbon dioxide.

-capnia   (condition of) carbon dioxide content in the blood.

caps-   capsule or container.

caput   head.

carb-   denoting carbon; carbonic; carboxyl.

carbo-   carbon, charcoal.

carbol-   denoting phenol.

carbon-   carbon, charcoal.

carcin-   cancerous, cancer.

-carcinoma   a malignant tumor composed of epithelial cells, with a tendency to metastasize.

card-   heart.

-cardia   a type of heart action or location.

-cardia   denoting a state or condition of the heart.

cardia-	heart.
-cardiac	1. to characterize types and locations of heart ailments; 2. to identify heart ailment patients.
cardio-	heart.
-cardium	denoting a structural layer of the heart or a membrane associated with the heart.
carneo	flesh.
carp-	carpals.
-carp	fruit.
carp-	wrist bones.
-carpal	wrist.
carpo-	denoting carpus, carpal.
caryo-	nucleus.
case-	casein; caseous.
caseo-	casein; caseous.
cat-	(prefix) downward; in accordance with; against, back; completely.
cat-	down, under, against, with.
cata-	(prefix) downward; in accordance with; against, back; completely.
cata-	down, under, against, with.

C

-catalytic   pertaining to a chemical reaction caused by an agent unchanged by the reaction.

cath-   (prefix) downward; in accordance with; against, back; completely.

-cathartic   pertaining to cleaning.

caud-   tail.

caudo-   caudal, tail.

caus-   burn, burning.

cauter   burn, heat.

cauter-   heat, burn.

cav-   hollow.

cec-   cecum.

ceci-   cecum.

ceco-   cecum.

cel-   cavity of the body; swelling or tumor.

-cele   denoting a chamber, a ventricle, or a normal cavity of.

-cele   tumor; hernia; pathologic swelling.

celi-   abdomen, belly.

celio-   abdomen, belly.

cell-   cellulose.

cello-	celluose.
cellul-	cell, cellular.
celluli-	cell, cellular.
cellulo-	cell, cellular.
cen-	general; common.
ceno-	general; common.
ceno-	new.
cente-	puncture.
-centesis	surgical puncture to remove fluid.
centi-	hundredth.
centri-	center.
centro-	center.
cephal-	head.
-cephalia	(condition of the) head.
-cephalic	relating to the head.
-cephalus	denoting an individual with a specified abnormality of the head or the abnormality itself.
-cephaly	a (specified) condition of the head.
cer-	wax.
cerato-	cornea; hornea tissue.
cerebell-	cerebellum.

C

cerebr-	cerebrum (largest part of the brain).
-cerebral	referring to the brain.
cervic-	neck (of the body or of the uterus).
cervico-	neck.
chalc-	copper; brass.
chalco	copper, brass.
cheil-	lip.
cheilo-	lip.
cheir-	hand.
cheiro-	hand.
-chelia	(condition of the) lips.
chem-	drug, chemical.
chemi-	chemical, chemistry.
chemico-	chemical, chemistry.
chemo-	chemical, chemistry.
-chezia	defecation, elimination of wastes.
chiasm	crossing.
chin-	quinine.
chino-	quinine.

-chiria	1. a (specified) condition involving the hands; 2. a (specified condition involving stimulus and its perception.
chlor-	green, pale green; chlorine.
chlorhydr-	hydrochloric acid.
-chloric	referring to or containing chlorine.
chloro-	green, pale green; chlorine.
chol-	gall, bile.
chole-	bile.
cholecyst-	gallbladder.
cholesterol-	cholesterol (a lipid substance).
-cholia	(condition of the) bile.
cholo-	bile.
chondr-	cartilage (type of connective tissue).
-chondria	condition involving granules in cell composition.
-chondroma	a benign cartilaginous tumor.
chord-	cord; notochord.
chord-	string, cord.
chordo-	cord; notochord.
-chorea	(specified) nervous disorder.

C

chori-   chorion.

chorio-   protective fetal membrane.

-chorion   a membrane.

chorion-   chorion.

-chroia   (condition of) coloration.

-chroia   coloration.

chrom-   color, colored; pigment, pigmented; chromium.

-chromasia (condition of) color (as cells, skin).

-chromasia denoting the condition or property involving color or color perception.

chromat-   color; pigment; chromatin.

-chromatic staining properties of tissues and microorganisms.

chromato- color.

-chrome   1. coloring substance within a cell or chemical compound; 2. a combining form distinguishing chromium alloys.

-chrome   colored.

-chromemia (condition of) the hemoglobin in the blood.

-chromia	state of pigmentation; a state involving color perception.
-chromic	(specified) number of colors seen by the eye.
chromo-	color.
chron-	time.
-chronia	(condition of) processes with respect to time.
chrono-	time.
chrys-	denoting gold, golden, golden yellow, yellow.
chryso-	denoting gold, golden, golden yellow, yellow.
chyl-	denoting chyle.
chyli-	denoting chyle.
-chylia	(condition of) the digestive juices.
chylo-	chyle.
-chymia	(condition of) partly digested food in the duodenum.
cib-	meals.
-cide	denoting killer; killing.
cili-	denoting cilia; ciliary.
cili-	eyelid.

C

cilio-   denoting cilia; ciliary.

cine-   movement.

circum-   around.

cirs-   meaning swollen vein, varix, varicose.

cirso-   meaning swollen vein, varix, varicose.

cis-   (prefix) on this side, on the same side; in chemistry, having certain atoms or groups of atoms on the same side of a molecule.

cis-   to cut.

clas-   a piece broken off.

-clasia   (specified) condition involving crushing or breaking up.

-clasis   denoting breaking, breaking up.

-clast   something that breaks.

-clastic   causing disintegration.

-clasty   denoting breaking, breaking up.

clavic-   clavicle.

clavicul-   clavicle (collar bone).

cleid-   denoting clavicle, clavicular.

cleido-   denoting clavicle, clavicular.

-cleisis	meaning closure.
cleist-	closed.
cleisto-	closed.
-clinic	places set aside for medical treatment.
clino-	to bend or make lie down.
-clinous	pertaining to ancestry.
clist-	closed.
clisto-	closed.
-clonia	(condition involving) spasms.
-cnemia	(condition of) the leg below the knee.
coagul-	clotting.
cocc-	denoting grain, seed; coccus.
-cocci	(plural of –coccus) berry shaped bacterium.
cocco-	denoting grain, seed; coccus.
cocco-	spherical bacterial cell.
-coccus	berry shaped bacterium.
coccy-	denoting coccyx.
coccyg-	coccyx (tailbone).
coccygeo-	denoting coccygeal; coccygeus.
coccygo-	coccyx.

C

coccygo-	denoting coccyx.
cochle-	cochlea.
cochlea	snail shaped.
coel-	cavity of the body.
coel-	colon.
-coele	denoting a chamber, a ventricle, or a normal cavity of the body.
coeli-	abdomen, belly.
coelio-	abdomen, belly.
coeno-	general; common.
col-	colon (large intestine).
colo-	colon.
-coloboma	absence or defect of an ocular tissue affecting function, especially of the iris.
colon-	colon.
colon-	colon.
-colon	the part of the large intestine between the cecum and the rectum.
-colonic	relating to the colon.
-color	hue or hues.
-colous	meaning inhabiting, growing in.

colp-	vagina.
colpo-	vagina.
-colpos	denoting vagina.
com-	(prefix) with, jointly, together.
-coma	1. (condition of) profound unconsciousness 2. (condition of) tarpor.
comat-	deep sleep (coma).
-comma	piece of a structure.
con-	(prefix) with, jointly, together.
-condyle	knucklelike projection on a bone.
coni-	dust.
-conia	small particles in the (specified) fluid or part of the body.
conjunctiv-	conjunctiva.
contra-	against, opposite.
copr-	feces.
copro-	feces.
cor-	(prefix) with, jointly, together.
cor-	pupil (of the eye).
coraco-	coracoid, coracoid process.
core-	pupil (of the eye).

C

-coria	1. (condition of the) sense of satiety; 2. (condition of the) pupil.
-cormia	an abnormal development of the trunk of the body.
corne-	cornea.
-cornea	condition of the cornea.
coro-	pupil of the eye.
coron-	heart.
corpor-	body.
cortic-	cortex, outer region.
cost-	ribs (true ribs, false ribs, and floating ribs).
costo-	rib.
counter-	(prefix) against, opposing; opposite.
cox-	hip, hip joint.
crani-	cranium (skull).
-crania	denoting (a specified) kind or condition of the skull or head.
-cranium	referring to the skull.
cras-	mixture.
-crasia	1. (condition of a) mixture, good or bad.

-cratia	(condition of) incontinence.
creat-	flesh.
cresc-	to grow.
crico-	denoting cricoid.
crico-	ring.
crin-	to secret (to form and give off).
crin-	to separate.
-crinia	(condition of) endocrine secretion.
-crisia	1. a diagnosis; 2. a (specified) condition of endocrine secretion.
crur-	leg.
cry-	cold, freezing.
crym-	denoting cold, frost.
cryo-	denoting cold, frost.
crymo-	cold, freezing.
crypt-	hidden.
crypto-	hidden.
crystal-	meaning crystal.
crystallo-	meaning crystal.
cub-	denoting cube; cubital; cuboid.
cubi-	denoting cube; cubital; cuboid.
cubo-	denoting cube; cubital; cuboid.

C

culd-	cul-de-sac.
cult-	to tend or cultivate.
cune-	denoting cuneiform.
cune-	wedge.
cupr-	copper.
cupro-	copper.
-current	running, flowing, happening.
-cusis	hearing.
cut-	pertaining to the skin.
cutane-	skin.
cyan-	dark blue; in chemistry the presence of a cyanogen group.
cyano-	dark blue; in chemistry – the presence of a cyanogen group.
cycl-	ciliary body or muscle of the eye.
cycl-	circle, circular.
cycl-	round, recurring.
cyclo-	round, recurring.
cyesio-	pregnancy.
-cyesis	pregnancy.
cylinder-	cylinder.
cylindro-	cylinder.

cymbo-	boat-shaped.
cyn-	dog.
cyno-	dogs, dog-like.
-cyst	bladder.
cyst-	gallbladder; urinary bladder.
-cyst	pouch or bladder.
cyst-	sac of fluid.
cyst-	urinary bladder; a sac or a cyst (sac containing fluid).
cysti-	gallbladder; urinary bladder.
-cystitis	inflammation of the bladder or cyst.
cysto-	gallbladder; urinary bladder.
cysto-	bladder, cyst or sac.
-cystoma	cystic tumor.
cyt-	cell, cellular, cytoplasm.
-cythemia	condition regarding cells in the blood.
cyto-	cell, cytoplasm.
-cytoma	a neoplasm made up of cells.
-cytosis	abnormal condition of cells.

D

dacry- tears, tear duct (see also lacrim-).

dacryo- tears.

-dactyl digit (finger or toe).

dactyl- fingers, toes.

-dactylia (condition of the) fingers or toes.

dactylo- finger or toe.

de- down, lack of.

dec- ten.

deci- denoting tenth; a measure one-tenth as large as the unit.

dem- denoting people, population.

dema- denoting people, combination.

demi- (prefix) half.

demon- denoting demon.

demono- denoting demon.

dendr- tree, branches.

-dendria trees, branches

-dendron tree-like formation.

dent- twig-like branching of nerve fibers. denoting tooth, dental.

denta- tooth.

dentate- meaning dentate. possessing teeth.

denti-	denoting tooth, dental.
dentia-	tooth.
dento-	denoting tooth, dental.
deoxy-	deoxidized or reduction product of.
der-	pertaining to the neck.
derm-	denoting integument; germ layer.
derm-	skin.
derma-	denoting dermis, dermal; skin, cutaneous.
-derma	kind of skin or integument; an abnormal condition of the skin.
dermat-	skin.
-dermia	(specialized) skin condition.
-dermic	related to the skin.
-dermis	tissue, skin.
dermo-	denoting dermis, dermal; skin, cutaneous.
des-	(prefix) reversing or undoing (of an action).
-desis	to bind, tie together.
-desma	something bridging or connecting.
desmo-	pertaining to a ligament.

D

deut-	second, secondary.
deuter-	second; secondary.
deuteron-	second; secondary.
deuto-	second, secondary.
deuto-	second.
dextro-	right.
di-	(prefix) through, across, between.
di-	(prefix) two, double.
dia-	(prefix) through, across, between, complete.
diaphor-	profuse sweating (see hidr-).
diaz-	signifying the presence (in an organic compound) of two nitrogen atoms.
diazo-	signifying the presence (in an organic compound) of two nitrogen atoms.
dicty-	network, net-like, reticular.
dictyo-	network, net-like, reticular.
didym-	testis.
-didymus	a pair of twins jointed at a (specified) part of the body.
dipl-	double.

diplo-	double.
dips-	thirst.
-dipsia	(condition of) thirst.
dis-	(prefix) two, double.
dis-	reversal or separation.
disc-	disk.
disco-	disc, disc-shaped.
disco-	disk.
dist-	far, distant.
disto-	distal.
dolich-	denoting long; narrow.
dolicho-	denoting long; narrow.
dors-	back portion of the body.
-dorsal	the back of something, back.
dorsi	back.
dorso-	dorsum, back.
drom-	course; running; speed.
-drome	that which runs in a specified way.
dromo-	course; running; speed.
dromo-	running, conduction.
duct-	to lead, carry.
duo-	two.

D

duoden- duodenum.

duodeno- duodenum.

dur- dura mater.

-dymia an abnormal condition of anomalous twins joined at part of **their** bodies; conjoined, duplicity.

-dymus superior duplicity.

dynam- power, energy, motion.

-dynamia strength; a condition of having strength.

dynamo- pertaining to power or strength.

-dynia pain.

dys- (prefix) difficult, painful.

-dysplasia (condition of) abnormal development.

e-	(prefix) out, away, off.
-eal	pertaining to.
ec-	(prefix) out; outside of.
ec-	out of.
ec-	out, outside.
-echia	condition of holding.
echin-	spiny.
echino-	spines, spiny.
echo-	a repeated sound.
-ecoia	(condition of the) sense of hearing.
-ectasia	(condition of) dilation, extension, or distension of an organ.
ecto-	out, outside. for excising.
-ectomy	excision, removal, resection.
-ectomy	surgical removal of something specified.
-ectopia	condition in which a (specified) organ or part is out of its normal place.
ectro-	congenital absence.
ede-	pertaining to the external genitals.

E

-edema swelling resulting from an excessive accumulation of serous fluid in the tissues of the body in (specified) locations.

edeo- pertaining to the external genitals.

edo- pertaining to the external genitals.

ef- (prefix) out, away, off.

electro- electricity.

eleo- oil.

em- (prefix) in, inside, into.

-ema condition.

embry- embryo, fetus.

embryo- embryo, fetus.

-emesis vomiting.

-emia denoting (specified) condition of the blood or presence in the blood of a (specified) substance.

-empyema accumulation of pus, especially thoracic.

en- (prefix) in, inside, into.

encephal- brain.

-encephalia (condition of the) brain.

-enchyma   the liquid that nourishes tissue, or tissue itself, enclosing a part or affecting the tissues around a part.

-ency   quality or state, person or thing in a state.

end-   inner, internal.

endo-   inner, internal.

-endothelioma   a tumor of endothelial tissue.

ent-   within; inner.

enter-   intestines (usually the small intestines).

entero-   intestines (usually small intestines).

ento-   within; inner.

eosin-   red, dawn, rosy.

ep-   (prefix) upon, beside, above; in chemistry, relation of some kind to a (specified) compound.

epi-   (prefix) upon, beside, above; in chemistry, relation of some kind to a (specified compound.

epididym-   epididymis.

epididymo   epididymis.

epiglott-   epiglottis.

E

epiplo-   denoting epiploon or omentum.

episi-   vulva.

episio-   vulva.

equi-   equal, equality.

-er   one who.

erg-   work; activity.

-ergasia   interfunctioning of the mind and body.

-ergic   an effect of activity.

ergo-   pertaining to work.

-ergy   1. an action; 2. an effect or result.

erot-   sexual desire.

-erotic   pertaining to sexual love or desire.

eroto-   love, sexual desire.

erythem-   redness.

erythemat-   redness.

erythr-   red.

erythro-   red.

erythrocyte-   erythrocyte.

-escence-   (suffix) a process of becoming; likeness, similarity.

-escent   (suffix) becoming; like, somewhat.

-escent	beginning to be.
-esis	(suffix) action; process.
-esis	action, process, or result of.
eso-	(prefix) inner.
esophag-	esophagus, esophageal.
esophago-	esophagus, esophageal.
esthes	feeling, sensation.
esthesi-	feeling, nervous sensation.
-esthesia	a condition involving sensation or sense perception.
esthesio-	feeling, perceptive faculties.
esthesio-	sense, sensory, sensation.
-esthetic	pertaining to a person's consciousness of something.
estr-	female.
ethmo-	ethmoid.
-etic	a combing form used as the equivalent of –ic in forming adjectives.
eu-	good, normal.
eu-	well, easily, good.
eury-	broad, wide.
ex-	(prefix) out, away, off.

E

ex-	away from, outside, without.
ex-	out, away from.
ex-	outside; outside layer; out of.
exo-	outside; outside layer; out of.
extra-	(prefix) outside of; beyond the scope of.
extra-	outside of, beyond, in addition to.

faci-	face.
facio-	face.
-faction	a process of making.
-factive	making.
fasci-	fascia (forms sheaths enveloping muscles).
fascio-	fascia, fascial.
-fast	securely attached; resistant to a (specified) dye.
febri-	fever.
-febrile	pertaining to fever.
femor-	femur (thigh bone).
-fer	something that carries something.
-ferous	producing or carrying something specified.
ferr-	pertaining to iron.
ferri-	ferric, containing iron as a trivalent element.
ferro-	ferrous; containing metallic iron.
feti-	fetus, fetal.
feto-	fetus, fetal.
fibr	fibers.
fibrin-	fibrin, fibrinous.

F

fibrino-   fibrin, fibrinous.

fibro-   fiber.

-fibroma   a benign tumor made up of fibrous tissue.

-fibrous   composed of fibrous tissue.

fibul-   fibular (smaller lower leg bone).

fila-   thread, threadlike.

fiss-   split, cleft.

flagell-   whiplike process, tapping.

flav-   yellow.

-flect   to bend.

flex-   bend.

-fluent   flowing.

fluor   luminous, fluorescence.

foeti-   fetus, fetal.

follicul   small glandular sacs.

-footed   having feet of a specific sort for food.

for-   opening.

fore-   before, preceding; in front, anterior.

-form   having the form of, shaped, resembling.

forto-	fetus, fetal.
fract-	breaking.
front-	pertaining to the forehead, or front.
fronto-	frontal; forehead.
-fugal	tending to act in a direction away from.
-fuge	that which causes to flee, or drives away.
fung	fungus, mushroom.
furc-	forking, branching.
-fuse	to pour or flow.
fusi-	spindle; fusiform.
fuso-	spindle; fusiform.
-fy	to make into something specified.

G

galact-   milk; milky fluid.

galacta-   milk.

galacto-   milk; milky fluid.

galvano-   denoting galvanic or direct current of electricity.

gam-   marriage; in biology, sexual union; in botany, union or fusion of parts.

gamet-   reproductive cell.

gameto-   reproductive cell.

gamo-   marriage; in biology, sexual union; in botany, union or fusion of parts.

-gamy   a specified type of marriage or sexual union.

gangli-   ganglion.

ganglio-   ganglion.

-gaster   belly, abdomen; stomach.

gastr-   stomach, abdomen.

-gastria   condition or kind of stomach.

-gastric   a type of stomach or number of stomachs.

gastro-   stomach, abdomen.

ge-	denoting earth, ground; geographic.
gelat-	to freeze, congeal.
gemin-	twin, double.
-gen	1. that which generates; 2. that which is generated.
gen-	gene, genetic; genital, sexual.
gen-	to become or produce.
-gen	substance or organism that produces or generates; a thing produced or generated.
-gene	substance or organism that produces or generates; a thing produced or generated.
-genesia	1. a (specified) condition concerning information; 2. the production or procreation of something (specified).
-genesis	condition of producing, forming.
-genesis	formation.
-genesis	formation.
-genetic	1. pertaining to generation by (specified) agents;
geni-	chin.

G

-genia	(condition of development of the) jaw.
-genic	pertaining to producing, produced by, produced in.
-genic	producing, forming; produced by, formed from.
genio-	chin.
genito-	combining form meaning genital.
geno-	gene, genetic; gential, sexual.
-genous	meaning producing; produced by.
-genous	producing or produced by.
geny-	denoting under the jaw.
-geny	production, generation, origin.
genyo-	denoting under the jaw.
geo-	denoting earth, ground; geographic.
ger-	old age.
gera-	old age.
gerio-	old or aged.
-gerious	bearing, holding; conveying conducting.
gero-	old age, the aged.
geronto-	old age, the aged.

-gerous	bearing, characterized by.
-geusia	(condition of the) sense of taste.
-geusia	condition of the taste sense.
giganto-	huge.
gingiv-	gums.
gingivo	gum.
glauc-	gray.
-glea	a binding gelatinous medium.
gli-	glial cells.
gli-	gluey, gelatinous; glia, glial, neuroglia.
-glia	neuroglia of a specified kind or size.
glia-	neuroglia, gluey substance.
glio-	gluey, gelatinous; glia, glial, neuroglia.
-glioma	tumor arising from the neuroglia.
-globin	protein.
-globinuria	(condition involving) the presence of complex proteins in the urine.
glomerul-	glomerulus.
gloss-	tongue; language.
-glossa	tongue.

G

-glossia   condition of the tongue.

glosso-   tongue; language.

glott-   glottis.

gluc-   glucose, sugar.

gluco-   glucose.

gluteo-   gluteus; gluteal.

glyc-   sweet; sugar.

-glycemia   condition of sugar in the blood.

glycogen-   glycogen, animal starch.

glycol-   sweet; sugar.

gnath-   jaw, jaws.

-gnathia   condition of the jaw.

gnatho-   jaw, jaws.

gnathous-   possessing a (specified) kind of jaw.

gno-   to know, discern.

-gnomonic   signs or experience in knowing or judging (a condition).

-gnomy   science, means of judging something specified.

gnos-   knowledge.

-gnosia   (condition of) perceiving or recognizing.

-gnosis	denoting knowledge, cognition, perception, recognition.
-gnostic	sensing; knowing.
gon-	knee.
gon-	seed (greek gone, seed).
gon-	sexual, generative; seed, semen; genitalia.
goni-	corner, angle.
-gonic	agents, processes, results of generation, reproduction, including the sexual.
gonio-	corner, angle.
gono-	semen, seed.
-gony	birth, origin.
-gony	generation, reproduction.
gony-	knee.
gony-	knee.
-gram	drawing, writing, record.
granduli-	granule, grandular.
grandulo-	granule, grandular.
granul-	granule, grandular.
-granuloma	tumor-like mass or nodule of granulation tissue.

G

-graph	something written or recorded.
-graph	the product of drawing or writing.
graph-	writing –graph instrument for recording.
-grapher	one who writes about something specified.
-graphia	a psychological abnormality revealed through handwriting.
-graphia	writing characteristic of a (specified) psychologic disorder; condition characterized by (a specified kind of) markings or tracings.
grapho-	writing.
grapho-	writing.
-graphy	a kind of printing.
-graphy	process of recording.
-graphy	process of recording.
-graphy	writing, delineating; recording.
gravid-	pregnancy, pregnant.
-gravida	pregnant woman with (specified) quantity of pregnancies.
gymno-	nakedness.
gyn-	woman, female.

-gyne	(specified) female characteristics.
gyneco-	woman, female.
-gynic	relating to the human female.
gyno-	woman, female.
-gynous	pertaining to female characteristics.
gyr-	ring, circle.
-gyria	(condition of the) development of the convolutions of the cerebral cortex.
gyro-	ring, circle.

H

haem-	blood.
haema-	blood.
hallucin	hallucination, to wander in the mind.
hapl-	single.
haplo-	single.
hapt-	contact, touch; binding, attaching.
hapto-	contact, touch; binding attaching.
hect-	one hundred.
hector-	one hundred.
helc-	ulcer.
helco-	ulcer.
heli-	the sun; sunlight.
helic-	helix; spiral.
helico-	helix; spiral.
helio-	the sun; sunlight.
helminth-	helminth, worm.
-helminth	worm.
helmintho-	helminth, worm.
helo-	horny, studded; corn.
hem-	blood.
hemat-	blood.

-hematoma a swelling containing blood.

hemi- (prefix) half, partial; in biology and medicine, either the right or left half of the body; in chemistry, a combining ratio of one-half.

hemoglobin- hemoglobin.

hepat- liver.

-hepatia (condition of the) liver or its functioning.

hepatico- hepatic.

hept- seven.

hepta- seven.

heredo- hereditary.

heter- another.

heter- other, another; different; irregular, abnormal.

hetero- other, another; different; irregular, abnormal.

hex- six.

hexa- six.

hidr- sweat, perspiration.

hidro- sweat, perspiration.

hidro- sweat, sweat gland.

H

hier-	sacred.
hier-	sacrum.
hiero-	sacred.
hiero-	sacrum.
hipp-	horse, equine.
hippo-	horse, equine.
hist-	tissue.
-histechia	tissue retaining a (specified) substance.
histi-	web, web-like; tissue.
histio-	web, web-like; tissue.
histo-	tissue.
hod-	pathways.
hol-	complete, entire; homogeneous.
holo-	complete, entire; homogeneous.
holo-	entire, the whole.
hom-	common, like, same; in chemistry and biology, homologous.
homal-	level, even; equal.
homalo-	level, even; equal.
home-	sameness.
homeo-	sameness, similarity.

homo-	common, like, same; in chemistry and biology, homologous.
homoeo-	sameness, similarity.
homoio-	like, similar.
horm-	to urge or stimulate.
-hormone	chemical substance possessing a regulatory effect.
hormone-	hormone.
hyal-	glass, transparent; vitreous, hyaloids.
hyal-	resembling glass.
hyalo-	glass, transparent; vitreous, hyaloids.
hyalo-	resembling glass.
hydr-	water, hydrogen.
-hydria	level of fluid in the body.
hydro-	water, hydrogen.
hydroxyl-	indicating the hydroxyl group.
hygr-	moist, moisture.
hygro-	most, moisture.
hyl-	material, substance, matter.
hylo-	material, substance, matter.
hymen-	hymen; membrane.

H

hymeno-   hymen; membrane.

hyo-   hyoid.

hyp-   (prefix) deficiency, lack; below, beneath.

hyper-   (prefix) excessive; above normal; in anatomy and zoology situated above.

hypn   sleep.

hypn   sleep.

-hypnotic   pertaining to hypnosis.

hypo-   (prefix) deficiency, lack; below, beneath.

hypo-   deficient, below, under, less than normal.

hypsi-   high.

hypso-   height.

hyster-   uterus, womb.

hystero-   pertaining to the uterus.

-ia	(suffix) condition, especially an abnormal or pathologic condition.
-ia	condition.
-iac	pertaining to.
-ian	belonging to, characteristic of, similar to.
-iasis	(suffix) a diseased condition caused by or resembling.
-iasis	a disease produced by something specified; a disease producing specified characteristics.
-iasis	abnormal condition.
iatr-	treatment, physician.
-iatric	pertaining to medical treatment of (a specified category or aspect of patient(s).
-iatro	a relation to medicine or to physicians.
iatro-	treatment, physician.
-iatry	a specified type of medical treatment.
-ic	pertaining to, similar to.
-ical	pertaining to.
ichthy-	scaly, dry (fish-like).

I

ichthyo- fish.

icon- image.

icono- image.

-ics (suffix) a field of organized knowledge or practice.

-ics the systematic formulation of a body of knowledge.

icter- icterus, jaundice.

ictero- icterus, jaundice.

-id (suffix) a stage in the maturation of a kind of cell or organism.

-id a structural element of teeth.

-idae in biology, (suffix) taxonomic family.

-ide (suffix) the nonmetallic element in a binary compound.

-ide a combining form naming binary compounds composed of a metallic and a nonmetallic element.

-idene (suffix) a radical having two valence bonds at the point of attachment.

ideo- idea; pertaining to the mind.

-idin	chemical compound related in origin or structure to another compound.
-idine	chemical compound related in origin or structure to another compound.
idio-	denoting one's own; separate, distinct; self-produced.
idio-	self, something separate.
-idium	a noun-forming combining form.
-iform	having the form of, shaped, resembling.
-iform	in the form of.
-il	a substance related to another.
ile-	ileum, ileal.
ileo-	ileum, ileal.
ili-	ilium (upper part of the pelvic bone).
-iliac	pertaining to the ilium.
ilio-	ilium, flank.
im-	(prefix) in, into, on, onto.
im-	(prefix) not.

I

imin-   designating the bivalent group when attached to or in nonacid radicals.

imino-   designating the bivalent group when attached to or in nonacid radicals.

immun-   protection.

immune-   protection.

in-   (prefix) in, into, on, onto.

in-   (prefix) not.

-in   (suffix) product derived from a particular organism or substance .

-in   a combining form meaning an antibiotic; a pharmaceutical product; a chemical compound; an enzyme.

-in   a substance.

in-   fiber, fimbrous; muscle fiber, muscle.

-in   of or pertaining to fibers.

increto-   internal secretions.

incud-   anvil.

incud-   incus, incudal.

incudo-   incus, incudal

-ine	(suffix) pertaining to or –like.
-ine	a substance.
infeo-	inferior, below.
infra-	(prefix) below, beneath, inferior; within.
infra-	beneath.
inguin-	groin.
ino-	fiber, fibrous; muscle fiber, muscle.
insul-	island, island-shaped.
inter-	(prefix) between, among; mutual, reciprocal.
inter-	situated, formed, or occurring between.
intra-	into, within.
intro-	(prefix) inward, into.
intro-	into, within.
iod-	iodine; violet.
iodo-	iodine; ion concentration in the blood.
iodo-	iodine; violet.
-ion	(suffix) small.
-ion	electrically charged particle; a noun-forming combining form.

I

-ion	process.
ionto-	ion, ionic.
-ior	pertaining to.
ir-	iris (colored portion of the eye around the pupil).
irid-	iris (colored portion of the eye around the pupil).
irido-	iris, a colored circle.
irido-	iris.
is-	equality, similarity.
is-	same, equal.
isch-	to hold back.
ischi-	ischium (posterior part of pelvic bone).
ischi-	ischium, ischial.
ischio-	ischium, ischial.
ischio-	ischium, the hip.
-ism	condition of, practice of, theory of.
-ism	process, condition.
ismus-	(suffix) spasm, contraction, displacement.
-ismus	condition of, practice of, theory of.

iso-	equal.
iso-	equality, similarity.
-ist	(suffix) one who does, practices, or deals with.
-it is	inflammation of a (specified) organ.
-ite	(suffix) the salt or ester from an acid with the termination – ous.
-ite	compounds.
ithy-	straight.
-itic	of or related to something specified.
-itol	(suffix) denoting a polyhydroxy alcohol, usually related to a sugar.
ium	(suffix) chemical element; chemical radical; anion with a positive charge.
-ium	a combining form used to name metallic elements.
-ium	structure, tissue.
ixodi-	ticks.
-ize	do, treat, cause.

J

jeco-	liver.
jejun-	jejunum.
jejuno-	jejunum.
jug-	yoke.
jugu-	throat, neck.
juxta-	near.

kak-	bad.
kal-	potassium (an electrolyte).
kali-	potassium.
kaps-	capsule or container.
kary-	nucleus.
karyo-	nucleus.
kat-	down, against.
kata-	(prefix) downward.
kel-	of or pertaining to a tumor.
ken-	empty.
keno-	empty.
kera-	horn.
kerat-	cornea.
kerat-	hard, horny tissue.
kerauno-	of or pertaining to lightening.
ket-	in chemistry, the presence of the ketone group.
ket-	ketone bodies (ketoacids and acetone).
keto-	a combining form indicating possession of the carbonyl group.
keton-	ketone bodies (ketoacids and acetone).

K

kilo- (prefix) thousand.

kin- action, motion.

kine- action, motion.

kine- movement.

kines- movement.

kinesi- movement.

-kinesia (cf) denoting a condition involving movements.

kinesio- movement.

-kinesis an activation; division (of cells).

kinet- motion, movement, kinesis, kinetic.

-kinetic 1. pertaining to motion; 2. pertaining to a (specified) agent causing motion; 3. referring to kinesis; 4. referring to activation of a body part by a (specified) agent.

kineto- movable.

kino- action, motion.

klept- stealing, theft.

klepto- theft, stealing.

koilo- hollow, concave.

koinoni-	a community.
koly-	to hinder.
kon-	dust.
krymo-	denoting cold, frost.
krypto-	denoting hidden.
kymo-	of or pertaining to waves.
kymo-	waves.
kyno-	of or pertaining to dogs.
kyph-	humpback, hunchback (posterior curvature in the lumbar region).
kypho-	hump.

L

-labe	something that takes, removes, takes up, absorbs.
labi-	lip.
-labial	lips.
-labile	unstable, subject to change.
labio-	lip.
lachry-	tears.
lacri-	tears.
lacrim-	tears.
lact-	milk, lactone or sulfone.
lagen-	flasklike.
-lagnia	a sexual predilection.
lal-	talk, babble.
-lalia	disorder of speech.
lalio-	talk, babble.
lalo-	talk, babble.
lamin-	lamina (part of the vertebra arch).
lamin-	layer.
lampro-	clear.
lano-	wool.
lapar-	abdomen, abdominal wall.
laparo-	loin, flank.

-lapse	a slip.
laryng-	larynx, voice box.
laryngo-	larynx.
later-	side.
lecitho-	yolk of an egg, ovum.
leio-	smooth.
leiomy-	smooth (visceral) muscle that lines the walls of internal organs.
lemma-	a confining membrane.
lemo-	plague.
lepido-	flake or scale.
lepro-	leprosy.
-lepsy	seizure.
lept-	thin, slender.
-leptic	pertaining to a (specified) type of seizure.
-leptic	to seize hold of.
lepto-	thin, delicate.
leuk-	white.
-leukemia	an increased number of leukocytes in the tissues and/or in the blood.
leuko-	white corpuscle, white.
levo-	left.

L

lex-   word, phrase.

-lexia   impairment of reading; impairment of word recognition.

lien-   spleen, splenic.

lieno-   spleen, splenic.

lieno-   spleen.

ligament-   ligament.

lingu-   tongue.

lio-   smooth.

lip-   fat, lipid.

lip-   fat.

lip-   fat.

lipo-   fat.

lipo-   lack, absence.

-lipoma   tumor made up of fatty tissue.

-lipsis   to leave, fail, omit.

-listhesis   slipping.

-lith   a calculus.

lith-   stone.

litho-   stone.

lob-   lobe of the lung.

-lobe   rounded prominence.

loc-	place.
log-	word, speech; thought, reason.
loga-	whites of the eye.
-logia	a condition involving the faculty of speech or of reasoning.
logo-	word, speech; thought, reason.
-logy	a field of study; discourse, treatise.
-logy	a science.
-logy	process of study.
-logy	study of.
loph-	ridge.
lord-	curve, swayback (anterior curvature in the lumbar region).
loxo-	oblique.
luc-	light.
-lucent	light-admitting.
-lucent	to shine.
lue-	of or pertaining to syphilis.
-luetic	pertaining to syphilis.
lumb-	lower back (side and back between the ribs and the pelvis).
lumbo-	the loins.
lumi-	irradiation, fluorescence.

L

lumin-	luminosity.
lun-	moon.
lyco-	wolf.
-lymph	clear body fluid.
lymph-	lymph.
lymphaden-	lymph node (gland).
-lymphoma	a tumor or neoplastic disorder of lymphoid tissue.
lyo-	dissolution, dispersion.
lys-	lysis, dissolution, solution.
lysi-	lysis, dissolution, solution.
-lysin	cell-dissolving antibody.
-lysis	breaking down or detachment.
-lysis	destruction, breakdown, separation.
lyso-	lysis, dissolution, solution.
lyso-	of or pertaining to dissolution.
lysso-	rabies, hydrophobia.
-lyte	a substance capable of or resulting from decomposition.
-lyte	denoting a substance capable of undergoing lysis.
-lytic	meaning pertaining lysis or lysine.

-lytic   pertaining to destruction.

-lytic   pertaining to or effecting
decomposition.

-lyze   to produce decomposition.

M

macr-	large, great; long, length.
macro-	large, great; long, length.
mal-	abnormal.
mal-	bad.
-malacia	softening of tissue.
malaco-	abnormal softness.
malleol-	malleolus (process on each side of the ankle).
mamm-	breast.
man-	hand.
-mancy	divination in, through, or by.
mandibul-	mandible (lower jaw bone).
mani-	mental aberration; Mania.
-mania	a (specified) state of mental disorder.
-mania	obsessive, preoccupation.
-maniac	a person exhibiting a type of psychosis; person revealing an inordinate interest in something.
-manic	(specified) psychosis; a mental state like.
-massage	a therapeutic kneading of the body.

mast-	breast.
masto-	breast.
mastoid-	mastoid process.
maxilla-	maxilla (upper jaw bone).
-maxilla	the upper jaw or the bones composing it.
-mazia	(condition of the) breasts.
mazo-	of or pertaining to the breast.
meat-	meatus.
medi-	middle, medial, median, intermediate.
mediastin-	mediastinum.
medull	soft, inner part.
meg-	large, extended, enlarged.
mega-	large, extended, enlarged.
megalo-	great, huge.
-megaly	enlargement of a (specified) body part.
mego-	great, huge.
meio-	meaning reduced, rudimentary; contraction, constriction.
mel-	cheek.
mel-	limb, extremity, member.

M

melan-	black, dark; pertaining to melanin.
melano-	black, dark; pertaining to melanin.
meli-	sugar.
meli-	sweet, related to honey.
-melia	denoting a condition of the limbs or extremities.
-melia	sweet, related to honey.
melo-	cheek.
melo-	limb, extremity.
-melus	denoting an individual having (specified) abnormalities of the limbs.
memingo-	pertaining to membranes covering the brain or spinal cord or to other membranes.
-men	a condition or result of a (specified) action.
men-	menses.
men-	mensus, menstruation.
mening-	meninx, meninges; membrane, membranous.
meningi-	membranes, meninges.
meno-	menses.

ment-	mind.
-mentia	(condition of the) mind.
-mer	part, portion.
-mercuric	molecules of bivalent mercury or its components.
-meria	(condition of) parts.
mero-	part.
mes-	(prefix) and meaning mid-, middle, medial; mesentery.
meso-	middle.
met-	(prefix) signifying behind, beyond; between, among; change, transformation; after, post.
meta-	(prefix) signifying behind, beyond; between, among; change, transformation; after, post.
meta-	beyond; change.
metacarp-	metacarpals (hand bones).
metarars-	metarsals (foot bones).
-meter	denoting an instrument for measuring or recording.
-meter	instrument to measure.
metopo-	forehead.

M

metr-	measure.
metr-	uterus.
metra-	uterus.
metri-	uterus.
-metria	(condition of the) ability to measure muscular acts.
-metria	(condition of the) uterus.
metro-	uterus.
-metropia	(condition of the) refraction of the eye.
-metry	meaning science or process of measurement.
mi-	smaller, less.
micr-	small, minute; undersized, abnormally small; microscopic; one one- millionth.
micro-	small, minute; undersized, abnormally small; microscopic; one one-millionth.
micro-	small.
-microbe	a small living organism.
-microbic	referring to or consisting of microbes.
mid-	middle.

milli-	1/1000[th.]
milli-	denoting a thousand or a thousandth.
millimicro-	billionth.
-mimesis	simulation, imitation.
-mimetic	pertaining to simulation of (specified) effects.
-mimia	(condition of) ability to express thought through gestures.
mio-	less.
mio-	meaning reduced, rudimentary; contraction, constriction.
mis-	denoting hatred, hating.
miso-	denoting hatred, hating.
mit-	filament; mitosis.
mito-	filament; mitosis.
mito-	threadlike.
-mixis	a (specified) means of conjugation.
mne-	of or pertaining to memory.
-mnesia	(condition or type of) memory.
-mnesia	denoting a type or condition of memory.
-mnestic	pertaining to memory.

M

mogi-	difficult or with difficulty.
mon-	meaning single, one, alone.
mon-	one, single.
mono-	meaning single, one, alone.
mono-	one.
-morph	denoting a category of individuals.
morph-	form or structure.
-morph	something possessing a (specified) form.
-morphia	condition of form.
-morphic	having a (specified) form.
-morphism	condition of having a (specified) shape.
morpho-	form or structure.
-morphosis	development or change.
-morphosis	meaning formation or change of form.
-morphous	meaning having a (specified) form.
-morphy	denoting the condition or characteristic of having a (specified) form.
-morula	a clump of blastomeres formed by cleavage of a fertilized ovum.
mot-	movement.

motility	condition of being capable of movement.
-motor	pertaining to the effects of activity in a body part.
muc-	meaning pertaining to mucus; mucin; mucosa.
muci-	meaning pertaining to mucus; mucin; mucosa.
muco-	meaning pertaining to mucus; containing or composed of mucous.
multi-	many.
mut	genetic change.
mutagen	causing genetic change.
my-	muscle.
myc-	fungus (fungi includes yeasts, molds, and mushrooms).
-myces	meaning fungus.
mycet-	meaning fungus.
-mycete	meaning fungus.
myceto-	meaning fungus.
-mycin	denoting a substance derived from a fungus
myco-	fungus.

M

mydr-   widen, enlarge.

myel-   spinal cord (means bone marrow in other contexts).

-myelia   (condition of the) spinal cord.

myelo-   marrow.

-myia   meaning fly.

myl-   meaning molar.

mylo   meaning molar.

myo-   relating to muscle.

myocardi-   heart muscle.

myom-   muscle tumor.

myos-   muscle.

myria-   a great number.

myring-   eardrum, tympanic membrane (see also tympan-).

myringo-   tympanic membrane.

myx-   mucus.

myxo-   mucus.

-myxoma   soft tumor made up of primitive connective tissues.

nano-   denoting dwarfed or undersized; one-billionth.

nano-   small, smallness, dwarfism.

naphtha-   pertaining to naphthalene or its ring structure; stupor.

narco-   denoting narcosis, numbness, or stupor.

narco-   stupor, stuporous state.

nas-   meaning nose, nasal.

naso-   meaning nose, nasal.

naso-   nose.

nat-   birth.

natr-   denoting sodium or natron.

natr-   sodium (an electrolyte).

natro-   denoting sodium or natron.

ne-   meaning new, newly formed.

necr-   death (of cells or whole body).

necro-   death, corpse.

nect-   to bind, tie, connect.

-nema   threadlike stage in the development of chromosomes.

N

nemato-   pertaining to a nematode, or to a threadlike structure.

neo-   new.

nephr-   kidney.

nephro-   kidneys.

-nephroma   tumor of the kidney or area of the kidney.

neur-   nerves.

-neural   of or relating to a nerve or nerves.

-neure   nerve cell.

-neuria   a (specified) condition involving nerves.

neuro-   nerves.

-neuroma   tumor made up of nerve cells and fibers.

-neurosis   a disease of the nerves or a mental disorder.

-neurotic   pertaining to a (specified) abnormal condition of the nerves; pertaining to (psyco)neurosis.

neutr-   neutral (neither base nor acid).

neutr-   neutrophil (a white blood cell).

nitro-   nitrogen.

nitroso-	a combining form indicating presence of the group –n:o:.
noci-	denoting pain.
noct-	night.
nocti-	night.
nocto-	night.
noctu-	night.
nod-	knot.
-noia	(condition of the) mind or will.
-noma	spreading, invasive gangrene.
-nomia	aphasia involving names or naming ability.
nomo-	usage or law.
-nomy	received knowledge in a field.
non-	(prefix) meaning not.
non-	meaning ninth, nine, nine times.
non-	nine.
noo-	meaning mind or mentality.
nor-	(prefix) indicating removal from a parent compound of a radical (often methyl) to form another compound.
norm-	rule, order.

N

-normal	relating to a norm.
normo-	normal.
noso-	disease.
not-	back, dorsal.
noto-	back, dorsal.
nucle-	nucleus or nuclear.
-nuclear	of or referring to the nucleus.
nucleo-	nucleus.
nulli-	no, not, without.
nutria-	of or related to nourishment.
nyct-	night.
nycto-	night, darkness.
nymph-	nymphae, labia minora; female sexuality.
nympho-	labia majora.
nympho-	nymphae, labia minora; female sexuality.
nystagm-	nystagmus.
nystagmo-	nystagmus.
-nyxis	surgical puncture; paracentesis.

O

o-	egg.
ob-	against, in front of.
obstretr-	pregnancy and childbirth
oct-	eight.
octa-	eight.
octo-	eight.
ocul-	eye, ocular.
oculo-	eye, ocular.
-ode	a type of (specified) electrical conductor.
-ode	like a form of something specified.
-odont	having teeth of a (specified) kind.
odont-	teeth.
odont-	tooth; odontoid.
-odontia	condition or a treatment of teeth.
-odontic	pertaining to the size of teeth.
odonto-	teeth.
odonto-	tooth; odontoid.
-odyne	referring to, treating pain.
-odynia	a painful condition.
-odynia	a state of pain in a (specified) location.

O

odyno-   pain.

oesophag-   esophagus, esophageal.

oesophago-   esophagus, esophageal of two carbon atoms of the benzene ring, i.e., 1, 2-position.

-oi   a plural-forming element in borrowing from greek.

-oid   (suffix) like, resembling.

-oid   having the form or appearance of.

oiko-   house.

-ol   a combining form designating a member of the alcohol group.

-ol   an oil.

-ol   in organic chemistry, (suffix) denoting an alcohol, both characterized by thepresence of the oh group.

-ola   singular diminutive of the noun named.

-ole   (suffix) small.

ole-   oil; olein, oleic.

olecran-   olecranon (elbow).

oleo-   oil; olein, oleic.

olig-   few, scant; deficiency.

oligo-	few, scant; deficiency.
om-	shoulder.
oma-	shoulder.
-oma	tumor, mass, collection of fluid.
-oma	tumor, neoplasm.
-ome	(suffix) group, mass.
oment-	omentum.
omento-	omentum.
omo-	shoulder.
omphal-	navel, umbilicus.
omphalo-	navel, umbilicus.
omphalo-	of or related to the naval.
-on	an elementary atomic particle.
-on	(suffix) an elementary particle or quantum, as in electron, photon; functional unit, as in phron; an inert gas, as in neon.
onc-	tumor.
oncho-	tumor; bulk, volume; hooked, curved.
onco-	of or pertaining to a swelling, tumor or mass.
onco-	tumor; bulk, volume; hooked, curved.

O

-one	(suffix) in organic chemistry signifying a ketone or certain. other compounds that contain oxygen, as a combining form designating organic compounds.
-one	hormone.
oneir-	dream.
oneiro-	dream.
oneiro-	of or related to a dream.
-ont	cell, organism.
ont-	existence, an individual being,organism.
onto-	existence, an individual being, organism.
onych-	nail, claw.
-onychia	condition of the finger or toenails.
onycho-	nail, claw.
onycho-	of or related to the nails.
oo-	egg, ovum.
oophor-	ovary, ovarian.
oophoro-	ovary, ovarian.
-opaque	obscure.
-ope	a person having an eye defect.

-ophidia	venomous snakes.
ophthalm-	eye.
-ophthalmia	pathological or anatomical condition of the eye.
-ophthalmic	referring to, near, or for the eye.
-opia	a (specified) visual condition.
-opia	defect of the eye.
-opia	vision.
-opic	kind of vision or visual defect.
opistho-	backward, the back.
opo-	In pharmacology, juice.
-ops	in botany and zoology, meaning – eyed.
ops-	sight, vision.
-opsia	condition of vision.
-opsia	vision.
-opsy	examination; a condition of vision.
-opsy	process of viewing.
-opsy	to view.
opt-	denoting optic, vision, eye.
opt-	eye, vision.
-opter	measurement of vision.

O

opti-	visible, vision, sight.
optic-	eye, vision.
-optic	pertaining to vision.
optico-	visible, vision, sight.
opto-	denoting optic, vision, eye.
opto-	visible, vision, sight.
-opy	defect of the eye or in between, as specified by the prefix.
-or	(suffix) an agent, doer.
or-	mouth.
orch-	testis, testicle.
orchi-	of or pertaining to the testes.
orchi	testis, testicle.
orchid-	testis, testicle.
orchido-	testes.
orchio-	of or pertaining to the testes.
orcho-	testes, testicle.
-orexia	(condition of the) appetite.
-orexia	denoting condition of the appetite.
-organic	related to the internal organs of the body.
organo-	organ, organs.
organo-	organ; organic.

oro-	mouth.
orrho-	serum.
orth-	straight, upright.
orthi-	steep, upright.
orthio-	steep, upright.
ortho-	In chemistry, (prefix) indicating relationship.
ortho-	straight, normal, correct.
osche-	scrotum.
oscheo-	scrotum.
-ose	(suffix) carbohydrate.
-ose	(suffix) having, characterized by.
-ose	pertaining to, full of.
-osis	a (specified) action, process, or result.
-ous	pertaining to.
ov-	egg.
ovari-	ovary.
-ovaria	(condition of the) ovary or ovarial.
ovario-	ovary.
ovi-	egg, ova.
ovo-	egg, ova, ovum.

O

ovul-   egg.

ox-   oxygen.

oxa-   In chemistry, denoting the presence of oxygen in place of carbon.

oxal-   oxalic or oxalate.

oxalo-   oxalic or oxalate.

-oxemia   a (specified) state of oxygen in the blood.

-oxia   (condition of) oxygenation.

oxy-   sharp, pointed; keen, abnormally acute; acid;. containing oxygen or additional oxygen; containing hydroxyl.

oxy-   sharp, quick, sour, presence of oxygen in a compound.

-oyl   (suffix) denoting a radical formed from an organic acid when OH is removed from the latter, as the radical RCO- from RCOOH.

-pachy	denoting a condition involving thickening of a part or parts.
pachy-	thick, thickness; coarse; dura mater.
paed-	child.
paedo-	child.
-pagus	denoting a pair of conjoined twins joined at a (specified) site.
-pagy	denoting the state of conjoined twins at a (specified) site.
palat-	palate.
palato-	of or pertaining to the palate
palato-	palate, palatal, palatine.
paleo-	ancient; primitive, phylogenetically early; old.
pali-	(prefix) repetition or recurrence; again.
palin-	(prefix) repetition or recurrence; again.
pallido-	pallidal, globus pallidus.
palpebr-	eyelid.
pan-	all, every; in medicine, general, affecting all or many parts.
pancre-	pancreas, pancreatic.

P

pancreat-   pancreas.

-pancreatic   pancreas, a condition of the pancreas or adjacent organs.

pancreatico-   pancreatic.

pant-   all, whole.

panto-   all, whole.

papill-   optic disc; nipple-like.

papill-   papilla, papillary.

papillo-   papillary.

papulo-   papule, popular.

Par-   (prefix) near; beside, adjacent to.

par-   aside, beyond, apart from, against.

par-   other than, apart from.

par-   similar, beside.

para-   (prefix) near; beside, adjacent to.

-para   a woman who has given birth to children in a number of regnancies.

para-   abnormal, beside, near.

-para   denoting a woman who has borne a viable child or hildren for a designated time or number of times, a primipara (for the first time).

para- similar, beside.

para- (prefix) the relationship of two atoms in the benzene ring that are separated by two carbon atoms in the ring; Pertaining to the state in which the atomic nuclei of a diatomic molecule spin in opposite directions.

-paralytic pertaining to paralysis.

parieto- parietal.

-parous bearing, bringing forth.

-parous pertaining to the quantity of offspring produced simultaneously or to the method of gestation.

-parous producing or secreting; bearing offspring of a specified number, as biparous, or in a specified way, as oviparous.

part- childbirth.

-partite a combining form meaning having the (specified) number of parts.

parvi- meaning small, little; sometimes used instead of the more common micro.

patell- patella (kneecap).

P

-path   a (specialist) in a (specified) type of medical treatment; the individual suffering from a (specified) sickness or disease.

path-   disease.

-path   one suffering from a (specified) illness.

-pathetic   pertaining to emotions.

-pathia   disease, affection.

-pathic   affected by, depending on, pertaining to, or riginating in or caused by disease of a (specified) kind or art.

-pathic   referring to an illness or affected part of the body.

patho-   disease.

-pathy   disease condition.

-pathy   disease condition.

-pathy   suffering or illness.

pector-   chest.

pector-   of or pertaining to the breast.

ped-   child, foot.

-ped	creature possessing feet of a (specified) sort or quantity.
ped-	foot, pedal, hoof.
-ped	having (specified) number or kind of feet.
-pede	having (specified) number or kind of feet.
pedi-	foot, pedal, hoof.
pedia-	child, foot.
-pedia	compendium of knowledge.
-pedic	of or pertaining to children or their **treatment.**
-pedic	referring or pertaining to the feet.
pedo-	child, foot.
pedo-	child.
pedo-	foot, pedal, hoof.
pedo-	of or related to a child.
Pel-	mud.
pell-	skin.
-pellic	having a (specified kind of) pelvis.
pelo-	mud.
pelv-	pelvis (hipbone).
pelv-	pelvis.

P

Pelvi-	pelvis, pelvic.
pelvio-	pelvis, pelvic.
pelvo-	pelvis.
-penia	a (specified) deficiency.
-pennate	having feathers.
pent-	five.
penta-	five.
peps-	digestion.
-pepsia	a state of the digestion.
pept-	digestion.
Pept-	pepsin, peptic; peptone.
-peptic	pertaining to digestion.
pepto-	pepsin, peptic; peptone.
peptone-	peptone.
peptone-	peptone.
per-	throughout, completely.
per-	(prefix) throughout, completely, thoroughly; in chemisty, denoting the highest valence of.
peri-	(prefix) signifying about, beyond, around, near; especially.
peri-	around.
peri-	surrounding, around.

peri-	surrounding.
pericardi-	pericardium.
perineo-	perineum, perineal.
perineum-	perineum.
periost-	periosteum, periosteal.
perioste-	periosteum, periosteal.
periosteo-	periosteum, periosteal.
peritone-	peritoneum.
peritone-	peritoneum.
pero-	maimed or deformed.
Pero-	malformed, stunted, defective.
perone-	fibula.
-petal	moving toward, seeking.
petalo-	a leaf.
petr-	stone.
-pexis	a fixation of something specified.
-pexy	fixation, put in place.
-pexy	In surgery, fixation.
phac-	lens of the eye.
phag-	eat, swallow.
-phage	eat, swallow.
-phage	something that eats the matter specified.

P

-phagia denoting a condition involving eating or swallowing.

-phagia eating of a substance.

-phagia eating, swallowing.

phago- eating, ingestion.

-phagous eating, subsisting on.

-phagy denoting (particular kind of) eating or an eating or swallowing of (a specific substance).

-phagy the practice of eating something specified.

phak- lens of the eye.

-phakia lens.

phalang- phalanges (finger and/or toe bones).

-phalangia a condition of the bones of the fingers or toes.

phalango- denoting phalanx, phalangeal.

phall- penis.

phallo- penis.

-phane a thing with a (specified) appearance.

-phane meaning a substance having a (specified) form or appearance.

Phaner-	visible; open.
phanero-	visible, apparent.
phanero-	visible; open.
pharmaceu-	drug.
pharmaco-	drug.
pharmaco-	of or related to drugs or medicine.
pharmacy-	chemical, drug.
-pharmic	related to drugs and medicinal remedies.
pharyng-	pharynx, throat.
pharyng-	throat.
-phasia	speech disorder.
-phasic	relating to a speech disorder.
-phasis	speech, utterance.
-phemia	a (specified) disorder of speech.
-phemia	speech disorder.
phen-	derivation from benzene.
-phene	a combining form denoting members of the phenol group.

P

-phenone   denoting an aromatic ketone that contains a phenyl or substituted phenyl group attached to an acyle group, as in acetophenone and benzophenone.

phenoxy-   combining form indicating the presence of a chemical group composed of phenyl and an atom of oxygen.

pheo-   dusky.

-pher   carrier.

-phil   (suffix) denoting a substance having an affinity for, as acidophil, having an affinity for acid stains.

phil-   attraction to, love.

Phil-   denoting love of or loving; affinity for or having an affinity for.

-phil   of that which combines with or is stained by.

-phile   (suffix) denoting a substance having an affinity for, as acidophil, having an affinity for acid stains.

-philia   attraction for (an increase in cell numbers).

-philia   meaning craving for, abnormal tendency toward; affinity for.

-philic	denoting having an affinity for.
philo-	denoting love of or loving; affinity for or having an affinity for.
-philous	having an affinity for.
-philous	having an affinity for; loving.
-phily	a fondness for something.
phleb-	vein, venous.
phlebo-	vein, veins.
phlebo-	vein, venous.
phleg-	of or related to inflammation.
phlogo-	of or related to inflammation.
phob-	fear, morbid dread.
-phobe	of or pertaining to fear or morbid dread.
-phobe	one having a phobia.
-phobia	abnormal fear.
-phobia	fear, dread.
-phobia	fear.-phobia fear (irrational and often disabling).
-phobic	exhibiting or possessing an aversion for or fear of (something).
phon-	sound, specifically to sound of the voice.

P

phon-	sound; speech, voice.
phon-	voice.
-phone	a device for transmitting sound.
-phone	sound-transmitting or recording instrument.
-phonia	denoting sound; vocal or voice impairment.
-phonic	sounds made in a (specified) part of the body.
phono-	sound, specifically to sound of the voice.
phono-	sound; speech, voice.
-phony	sound.
-phony	sound; vocal or voice impairment.
-phor	bearer, carrier.
phor-	bearing, carrying.
Phor-	carrying, transmission; bearing, supporting; directing, turning.
phor-	to bear.
phore-	a bearer or possessor.
-phore	bearer, carrier
-phoresis	carrying, transmission.

-phoresis   movement in a (specified) manner or medium.

-phoresis   transmission.

-phoria   (condition of the) visual axes of the eye.

-phoria   feeling, bearing.

-phoria   tendency; turning of the visual axis, as in exophoria.

-phoric   bearing, carrying.

phoro-   carrying, transmission; bearing, supporting; directing, turning.

-phorous   bearing, carrying.

phos-   light.

phosph-   phosphorous, phosphoric.

phot-   light.

phot-   light; photon; photographic.

-photic   pertaining to the ability to see at a (specified) light level.

photo-   light; photon; photographic.

-phragma   a septum or musculomembraneous barrier between cavities.

phren-   diaphragm.

phren-   mind.

P

phren-	mind; brain; diaphragm; phrenic nerve.
-phrenia	a disordered condition of mental activity.
-phrenic	the diaphragm or adjacent regions of the body.
phrenico	phrenic.
phreno-	mind; brain; diaphragm; phrenic nerve.
phthi-	decay, wasting away.
phthisio-	tuberculosis.
-phthisis	loss, diminution.
-phthongia	a condition of speech.
phyco-	algae, seaweed.
phyco-	seaweed.
phyl-	descent, group, evolutionary taxonomic group.
phyl-	guarding or preservation.
-phyll	a coloring matter in plants.
phyll-	leaf, leaf-like; chlorophyll.
phyllo-	leaf, leaf-like; chlorophyll.
phyllo-	leaves.
phylo-	descent, group, evolutionary taxonomic group.

P

phylo-	type, kind.
-phyma	a swelling tumor.
phys-	growing.
physic-	nature, physiology.
-physical	natural.
physico-	physical.
-physics	the science of the nature of something specified.
physio-	natural; physical; physiological.
physio-	nature, physiology.
-physis	growth, growing.
-physis	to grow.
physo-	air, gas.
physo-	denoting presence, accumulation, or formation of gas.
Phyt-	denoting plant, vegetable.
phyt-	plant.
-phyte	a plant that grown in or on or produces.
-phyte	denoting plant; a pathological growth.
phyto-	denoting plant, vegetable.
phyto-	plant, plants.

115

P

pico-	one trillionth.
picro-	bitter.
piez-	pressure.
pil-	hair.
pilo-	resembling or composed of hair.
pimel-	denoting fat, fatty.
pimelo-	denoting fat, fatty
pimelo-	fat.
pio-	fat.
pituit-	phlegm.
-placenta	an organ shaped like a flat cake.
plagi-	oblique.
plagio-	oblique.
-plakia	patches on mucous membranes.
plan-	wandering, straying.
plani-	flat, level.
plano-	flat, level.
plano-	wandering, straying.
plano-	wandering.
plant-	sole of the foot.
plas-	formation, development.
plas	formation.

-plasia	(condition of) formation or development.
-plasia	denoting formation, development.
-plasia	development, formation, growth.
-plasia	formation, growth.
-plasis	molding.
-plasm	cell or tissue substance.
-plasm	denoting formed material; formative material.
-plasm	formation, growth.
plasm-	plasma; protoplasm; cytoplasm.
-plasma	denoting formed material; formative material.
-plasma	fluid part of cytoplasm or protoplasm.
plasma-	liquid portion of blood.
plasmo-	of or related to plasma.
plasmo-	plasma; protoplasm; cytoplasm.
-plast	a primitive cell.
plast-	formed.
-plast	primitive or formative organized unit of living matter, as a granule, organelle, or cell.

P

-plastia (condition of) cell or tissue formation or development.

-plastic formative, developmental.

-plastic pertaining to the development of something specified.

plasto- cytoplasm; plastid; development.

-plasty plastic surgery on a (specified) body part or by (specified) means.

-plasty surgical repair.

-plasy denoting formation, development.

platy- broad, fat.

ple many, more.

-plegia a (specified) paralysis.

-plegia paralysis.

-plegic of or pertaining to a specific paralysis.

-plegic paralyzed; pertaining to paralysis.

plei- multiple; excessive, extra.

pleio- more.

pleio- multiple, excessive, extra.

pleo- more.

pleo- multiple; excessive, extra.

pleon- multiple; excessive, extra.

pleur-	denoting side, lateral; pleurisy.
pleur-	pleura, side, rib.
pleur-	pleura (membrane surrounding lungs and adjacent to chest wall.
pleuro-	denoting side, lateral; pleurisy.
pleuro-	pleura, side, rib.
-plex	network.
plex-	stroke, strike.
-plexia	(condition resulting from a) stroke.
plic-	fold or ridge.
-ploid	(suffix) indicating a given multiple of or relationship to the haploid number of chromosomes, as diploid, heteroploid.
-ploid	having a (specified) number of chromosome sets.
-ploidy	the condition of having a (specified) number of chromosome sets.
pluri-	meaning several, being or having more than one.
pluri-	more.
-pnea	breath, breathing.

P

-pnea	breathing.
-pnea	denoting respiration, respiratory condition.
pneo-	breath, breathing.
pneo-	breathing, respiration.
pneum-	air, lung.
pneuma-	air, gas, respiration.
pneumato-	air, gas, respiration.
pneumo-	lungs, air, breath.
pneumon-	air, lung.
-pneumonia	an inflammation of the lungs.
pneumono-	lung.
pneumono-	lungs, air, breath.
-pnoea	denoting respiration, respiratory condition.
-pod	denoting having feet of a particular number or kind; foot or part resembling a foot.
pod-	foot or foot-like process.
-poda	In zoological taxonomy, meaning having feet of a particular number or kind.
-podia	endoting a condition of the feet.

-podium	something foot-like.
podo-	foot or foot-like process.
-podous	having feet of a particular number or kind.
-poeisis	production, making, forming.
-poetic	referring to production of something specified.
-poiesis	formation.
-poiesis	production of.
-poietic	producing something specified.
-poietic	producing, formative.
poikil-	varied, irregular.
poikilo-	irregular, abnormal, variable, usually with respect to size or shape.
poikilo-	varied, irregular.
poli-	gray; gray substance, gray matter.
polio-	gray matter in the nervous system.
poly-	many, much.
polyp	polyp.
pono-	pain.
pont-	bridge; pons, pontine.
pont-	pons.

P

ponto-	bridge; pons, pontine.
por-	passageway, duct; pore, opening; cavity, tract.
-pore	opening.
-pore	passageway.
poro-	callus.
poro-	passageway, duct; pore, opening; cavity, tract.
-porosis	pore, passage.
porto-	portal.
-position	to put, set in place.
post-	after, behind.
post-	after, behind.
poster-	back, behind.
postero-	posterior part.
postero-	posterior.
pot-	drinking.
-pragia	quality of action.
-prandial	meal.
-praxia	condition concerning the performance of movements.
-praxis	a therapeutic treatment involving a (specified) method.

-praxis	act, activity; practice, use.
pre-	(prefix) before.
pre-	before, in front of.
pre-	before.
presby-	old age.
prim-	first.
primi-	first.
Pro-	(prefix) front, forward; prior, before; precursor; promoting, furthering.
pro-	before, forward.
pro-	first.
proct-	anus and rectum.
proct-	anus; rectum; anus and rectum.
proct-	rectum.
procto-	anus; rectum; anus and rectum.
procto-	rectum.
pros-	forward, anterior.
proso-	forward, anterior.
-prosopia	(condition of the) face.
prosopo-	face.
prostat	prostate gland.

P

prostate- prostate gland.

prot/o first.

prote- protein.

proteo- protein.

proto- first.

proxim- nearest.

prurit itching.

psammo- sand, sandlike material.

pseudo- false.

psor- itching.

psych- mind.

-psychic relation between mind and body.

psycho- mind.

-psychosis serious mental disorder.

psychro- cold.

-pterygium (specified) abnormality of the conjunctiva.

ptoma- corpse.

-ptosis drooping, sagging, prolapse.

-ptosis prolapse of an organ.

ptyalo- saliva.

-ptysis spitting of matter.

-ptysis	spitting.
-ptysis	spitting.
pub-	adult.
pub-	pubis (pubic bone); anterior portion of the pelvic or hipbone.
-pubic	frontal part of the pelvis.
pubo-	adult.
puer-	child.
pulmo-	lungs.
pulmon-	lung.
-pulmonic-	lungs.
-pulsion	action or condition of pushing.
punct-	a point, or like a point.
pupill-	pupil.
pupillo-	pupil.
pur-	pus.
purpur-	purple.
py-	pus.
pyel-	renal pelvis.
pyelo-	pelvis of the kidney.
pygo-	buttocks.
pykno-	thick, compact, dense.

P

pyle-	portal vein.
pylor-	pyloric spincter.
pylorio-	pylorus.
pyo-	pus.
pyret	fever.
pyreto-	fever.
-pyrexia	febrile condition.
pyro-	fire, heat, produced by heating.

quadr-	four.
quarti-	fourth.
-quin	antimalarial medicinal compounds from quinine.
quin-	quinine.
quinque-	five.
quint-	fifth, five-fold.

R

rachio-   spine.

radi-   radius (lower arm bone – thumb side).

radi   rays, x-rays.

radi-   root.

radi   x-rays.

radi-   x-rays.

radicul-   nerve root.

radio-   radiation, sometimes especifically to.

rect-   rectum.

Recto-   rectum, rectal.

ren-   kidneys.

reticule-   netlike.

retin-   retina.

retino-   retina, retinal.

retro-   behind, backward.

rhabd-   stick, rod; striped, banded, striated.

rhabdi-   rod-shaped, rod rhabdo-stick, rod; striped, banded, striated.

rhabdo-   rod-shaped, rod.

rhabdomy-	skeletal (striated) muscle connected to bones.
rheo-	electric current, a flow.
rheumat-	watery flow.
-rheumatic	relating to or exhibiting traits of.
rhigo-	cold.
rhin-	nose, nose-like structure.
-rhine	having a (specified) kind of nose.
rhino-	nose, nose-like structure.
rhizo-	root.
rhod-	red.
rhodo-	red.
rhomb-	rhomboid; rhomboencephalic.
rhyp-	filth.
-rhysis	flowing out.
rhytid-	wrinkle, wrinkled.
rhytid-	wrinkle.
roentgen	x-rays.
rost-	beak.
rot-	turned, to turn.
rrachia	(specied) foreign chemical substance.

R

-rrhachis	vertebral column; spinal cord.
-rrhage	bursting forth (of blood).
-rrhagia	fluid discharge of excessive quantity.
-rrhagic	condition of excessive fluid discharge.
-rrhaphia	sewing or suturing.
-rrhaphy	suture.
-rrhea	fluid discharge, flow.
-rrheic	a fluid discharge.
-rrhexis	rupture of a (specified) body part.
-rrhine	having a (specified) kind of nose.
-rrhinia	condition of the nose.
-rrhinus	nose, a condition of the nose.
-rrhoea	flow, discharge.
-rrhoeica	fluid discharge.
-rrhythmia	condition of the heartbeat or the pulse.
rub-	red.
rubr-	red; pertaining to the red nucleus.
rubri-	red; pertaining to the red nucleus.
rubro-	red; pertaining to the red nucleus.
sacchari-	sugar.

saccharo-	sugar.
sacr-	sacrum.
sacro-	sacrum.
salping-	eustachian tube, auditory tube.
salping-	fallopian tube.
salpingo-	tube, fallopian tube.
-salpinx	uterine tube.
sangui-	blood.
sanita-	health.
sapo-	soap.
sarc-	flesh, connective tissue.
sarco-	related to the flesh.
-sarcoma	malignant neoplasm.
saturn-	lead.
saur-	lizard, reptile.
scaph-	meaning scaphoid.
scapho-	boat-shaped.
scapula-	scapula (shoulder blade).
-scapula	shoulder blade, or a part of the shoulder blade.
scat-	excrement, feces, fecal.
scato-	dung, fecal matter.
scel-	leg.

S

-scelia	(condition of the) legs.
-schisis	cleft, split, fissure, splitting.
schisto-	split, cleft.
schisto-	split, fissured, cleft.
schiz	split, cleft.
schizo-	divided, related to division.
Schizo-	split, cleft.
scia-	shadows, especially internal structures as produced by roentgen rays.
scirrh	hard.
scirrho-	hard, related to a hard cancer or scirrhus.
scler-	hard, hardness; sclerosis, sclerotic; sclera, scleral.
sclera-	hard, often used in relation to the sclera.
sclera-	sclera (white of the eye).
sclero-	hard, often used in relation to the sclera.
-scleroma	induration, a hardening of the tissues.
-sclerosis	hardening.

scoleco-	worm.
scoli-	crooked, bent (lateral curvature).
scolio-	twisted or crooked.
scop-	to examine, observe.
-scope	instrument for visual examination.
-scopia	observation.
-scopy	process of visually examining.
-scorbic	the prevention of treatment of scurvy.
-scorbutic	scurvy.
scot-	darkness.
scot-	pertaining to darkness.
scoto-	darkness.
seb-	sebum (oily secretion from sebaceous glands).
-sect	to cut.
sect-	to cut.
secund-	second.
-seme	(one) having an orbital index of less than 84, more than 89.
semeio-	sign, symptom.
semi-	one-half.
semin-	semen, seed.

S

sens-	perception, feeling.
seps-	decay.
seps-	infection.
-sepsis	decay due to a (specified) cause or of a (specified) sort.
sept-	nasal septum.
sept-	septum, septal.
sept-	seven.
septi-	septum, septal.
septi-	seven.
-septic	referring to decay of a sort or due to a (specified) cause.
-septicemia	(condition of the) blood caused by virulent microorganisms).
septo-	septum, septal.
ser-	serum, serous.
seri-	serum, serous.
sero-	blood serum.
sero-	serum, serous.
sesqui-	one and a half.
set-	bristle.
sex-	six.
sexi-	six.

sial-	saliva, salivary.
sialaden-	salivary gland.
sialia-	(condition of the) saliva.
sialo-	saliva, salivary glands.
sicc-	dry.
sider-	iron.
sidero-	iron.
sigmoid-	sigmoid colon.
simil-	like.
sin-	hollow, cavity.
sinap-	mustard.
sinistro-	left, left side.
sinus-	sinus, cavity.
-sis	state of, condition.
-site	means or matter of nourishmentor life support, as in parasite.
-site	organism living inside another from which it derives sustenance.
-sitia	(condition of) appetite.
sito-	food.
skato-	dung, fecal matter.
skelet-	skeleton, skeletal.

S

skeleto-	skeleton, skeletal.
skia-	shadows, especially of internal structures as produced by roentgen rays.
-sol	a colloidal solution.
solar-	of or pertaining to the sun.
solar-	the sun.
-soluble	able to be dissolved.
-solve	to loosen.
-soma	body or portion of a body.
soma-	body.
somat	body.
somat-	body.
somat-	somatic.
-somatia	(condition of the) body, especially concerning the size.
-somatic	cause of effects on the body.
somato-	body.
-some	a body of a specialized sort.
-somia	(condition of) possessing body.
-somia	condition of the body or soma, as macrosomia.
somn-	sleep.

somni-	sleep.
-somnia	(condition of or) like sleep.
somno-	sleep.
-somus	an individual with a (specified) form or condition of the body.
-somus	fetal monster with a body.
son-	sound.
sono-	sound.
spano-	scanty, scarce.
-spasm	convulsion of a specific sort.
-spasm	sudden, involuntary contraction of muscles.
spasmo-	spasms.
-spasmodic	pertaining to or referring to a spasm.
spectr-	image.
spectro-	spectrum, spectral.
sperm-	spermatozoa, semen.
-sperm	a seed.
sperm-	spermatozoa.
spermat-	semen.
-spermia	(condition of) possessing or producing seed.

S

sphacel-	gangrene.
sphaero-	round, sphere.
sphen-	wedge, wedge-shaped; sphenoid (bone).
spheno-	wedge, wedge-shaped; sphenoid (bone).
spher-	globe, round.
-sphere	a spherical body.
sphero-	round, sphere.
-sphgmia	(condition of the) pulse.
sphygm-	pulse.
sphygmo-	pulse.
-sphyxia	pulse.
spin-	spine, backbone.
spini-	spine.
spino-	spine.
spinth-	spark.
spir-	a coil, or coiled.
spir-	breathing.
spir-	respiration.
spiro-	coil, spiral.
spiro-	respiration.

-splanchnic viscera, entrails.

splanchno- viscus, splanchnic nerve.

spleen- spleen.

splen- spleen.

-splenia condition of the spleen.

spleno- spleen.

spodo- waste material.

spondyl- (used to make words about conditions of the structure) dylic vertebrae.

spondylo- vertebra, spinal column.

spongio- like a sponge, related to a sponge.

-spongium a network of reticulum.

spor- spore.

-sporangium encasement of spores.

-spore reproductive element.

spori- spore.

sporo- spore.

squam- scale-like.

-stabile stable, resistant to change.

-stage (specified) phase.

-stalsis contraction in the alimentary canal.

S

stann-	tin.
staped-	stapes (third bone of the middle ear).
staphyl-	clusters.
staphyl-	resembling a bunch of grapes.
staphylo-	grape-like; pertaining to the uvula, or the whole soft palate; staphylococci.
staphylo-	grape-like; pertaining to the uvula; staphylococci.
staphylo-	resembling a bunch of grapes.
stas-	stopped, relation to standing or walking.
-stasia	(specified) condition involving the ability to stand.
-stasis	to stop, control.
-stat	a substance or device, for maintaining a process in a steady State.
-state	result of a (specified) process.
-static	arresting, inhibiting.
stato-	equilibrium or steady state.
steap-	fat.
stear-	fat.

-stearic	(specified) fat or fat derivatives.
stearo-	fat.
steat-	fat.
steato-	fat.
stell-	star.
steno-	contracted or narrowed.
steno-	narric or constricted.
-stenosis	tightening, stricture, narrowing.
ster-	solid structure.
sterco-	feces.
stere-	involving three dimensions; involving depth perception.
stereo-	solid, three dimensional, firmly established.
stern-	sternum (breastbone).
-sternal	sternum.
-sternia	(condition of the) sternum.
sterno-	the sternum.
steth-	chest.
stetho-	chest.
sthen-	strength.
-sthenia	power, strength.

S

stheno-   strength.

-sthenuria   (condition of) urination or of the specific gravity on urine.

stib-   antimony.

-stichia   condition involving rolls of eyelashes.

-stole   contraction, retraction, dilation of various organs.

-stoma   mouth, opening; having a (specified) kind of mouth.

stomat-   mouth.

stomato-   mouth.

-stomia   (condition of the) mouth.

stomo-   mouth.

-stomy   opening to form a mouth.

-stone   calculus in a human organ or duct.

strab-   squinting.

strati-   layer.

streph-   twisted.

strepho-   twisted.

strept-   twisted chains.

strepto-   twisted.

stri-   line, streak.

strio-	stria, striated.
-stroke	condition caused by or resembling an apoplectic stroke.
stroma-	a covering.
-stroma	supporting tissue of an organ.
-strophe	turning or twisting.
strophe-	twisting.
strum-	goiter, scrofula.
-style-	a bone attached to an interverbebra structure.
stylo-	like a stake or a pole.
Sub-	(prefix) under, beneath; less than, below.
sub-	below, under.
sub-	under.
sub-	under. Depreciation.
succ-	juice.
sud-	perspiration, sweat.
sudo-	perspiration, sweat.
sulfo-	generally indicating the presence of divalent sulfur.
sulfo-	group.
-sulfuric	compounds containing sulfur.

S

super-	(prefix) above, upon; extreme, in high degree.
super-	above.
-suppression	to stop.
supra-	above, upper.
-surgery	treatment of illness or deformity.
sursum-	upward, swelling or tumor.
sy-	union, association.
syl-	union, association.
sym-	(prefix) with, together.
sym-	together, with.
-symbolia	(condition involving) the ability to interpret symbols.
symphysi-	symphysis.
symphysio-	symphysis.
syn-	(prefix) with, together.
syncope-	to cut off, cut short.
syndesmo-	connective tissue, particularly the ligaments.
synov-	synovial membrane.
-synthesis	putting together, formation of.
syring-	long cavity, tube, tubular, as a sweat gland duct, a fistula.

syring-	tube, fistula.
syringe-	long cavity, tube, tubular, as a sweat gland duct, a fistula.
syringo-	tube, fistula.
-sytole	types and locations of the higher blood pressure measurement.

T

tabe-	wasting (away).
tacho-	speed.
tachy-	swift, rapid.
tact-	touch.
-tactic	exhibiting agent-controlled orientation or movement tactile sense.
taenia-	ribbon, band.
tal-	talus, talar, ankle.
talip-	club-footed.
talo-	talus, talar, ankle.
tapho-	the grave.
tars-	tarsals (bones of the hindfoot).
tarso-	the edge of the foot, the eyelid.
-tas	a noun-forming combining form.
taur-	bull; taurine.
tauro-	bull; taurine.
tauto-	same.
tax-	order, coordination.
-taxia	(condition of) impaired mental or physical control.
-taxis	(specialized) arrangement.
-technics	the art or mechanics of.

-technique	the skillful way in which something is done.
techno-	art.
-techny	the art or mechanics of (a specified area).
tecto-	roof-like.
teg-	cover.
tel-	complete.
tela-	a web or weblike structure.
-tela	weblike membrane.
tele-	far.
telo-	the end.
tempo-	time.
ten-	tendon.
tendin-	tendon.
-tene	a chromosome filament in meiosis.
tenia-	ribbon, band.
teno-	tendon.
-tention	condition of being held; condition of being stretched.
tephr-	ash-colored.
ter-	three or threefold.
terat-	monster.

T

terato-	monster.
tert-	(chemical prefix) meaning tertiary.
terti-	third.
test-	testis, testicle.
-tetanic	producing tetanus or tetany.
tetano-	tetanus.
tetart-	fourth.
tetart-	fourth; a quarter, quadrant.
tetarto-	fourth; a quarter, quadrant.
tetr-	four.
tetra-	four.
tetro-	four.
thalam-	thalamus.
thalamo-	thalamus, thalamic.
thalasso-	sea.
thanat-	death.
thanato-	death.
thanato-	death.
thec	sheath (of brain and spinal cord).
thec-	sheath (refers to the meninges).
thec-	sheath, as of a tendon.
-thecium	sack or container.

thel-	nipple.
-thelia	(condition of the) nipples.
-thelioma	tumor in a cellular tissue.
-thelium	layer of (specialized kind of) cellular tissue.
thely-	female.
theo-	god.
therapeut	treatment.
-therapeutic	medical treatment by (specialized) techniques.
-therapia	medical care.
-therapy	medical treatment of disease.
therio-	beasts.
-therm	animal with a (specialized) body temperature.
therm-	heat.
-thermia	state of body temperature.
thermo-	heat.
-thetic	put, place, set.
thigm-	touch.
thio-	sulfur.
thixo-	touch.
thorac-	chest.

T

-thoracic	chest.
thoraco-	chest.
-thorax	pleural cavity, chest.
threp-	nutrition.
thromb-	clot, clotting.
thrombo-	clot, thrombosis.
thym-	thymus gland.
-thymia	(condition of the) mind, will.
-thymia	mind.
thymo-	thymus gland.
-thyrea	condition of the thyroid gland.
thyro-	thyroid gland.
tibi-	tibia (shin bone).
-tic	pertaining to.
toc-	childbirth.
-tocia	conditions of labor.
-tocia	labor, birth.
toco-	childbirth or labor.
-tome	instrument for cutting.
-tome	instrument to cut.
-tomic	related to incisions or sections of tissues.

-tomy	incision, cutting into.
-tomy	process of cutting, incision.
-tomy	surgical incision.
-tonia	(condition or degree of) tonus of a sort or in a region of the body.
-tonic	quality of muscle contraction, tonus.
tono-	tone, tension.
tonsil-	tonsils.
tonsill-	tonsils.
-tony	condition of motor control.
took-	childbirth or labor.
top-	place, position, location.
-topia	(condition of) placement of organs in the body.
topo-	place.
tors-	twisted.
tox	poison.
-toxemia	(specified) toxic substance in the blood.
-toxia	condition resulting from a poison in a (specified) region of the body.
-toxia	poison.

T

-toxic	poison.
toxico-	poison, poisonous.
-toxin	poison.
toxo-	poison.
trache-	trachea, windpipe.
trache-	trachea, windpipe.
trachelo-	neck, necklike structure.
tracheo-	trachea.
trans-	across, through, over.
trans-	across, through.
trans-	across, through.
trauma-	wound, injury, psychic, physical.
traumat-	trauma, traumatic.
traumato-	trauma, injury, wound.
traumato-	trauma, traumatic.
-trema	hole, orifice, opening.
-tresia	opening.
-tresia	perforation.
-tresia	trauma, traumatic.
tri-	denoting three.
-tribe	an instrument for crushing or compression.

-tribe	surgical instrument used to crush a body part.
trich-	hair.
trich-	hair; filament.
-trichia	denoting a condition of the hair; hairiness.
-trichia	pathological condition of the hair.
tricho-	hair, filament.
trigon-	trigone (region of the bladder).
-tripsis	chafing of a body part by a surgical instrument.
-tripsy	crushing of a body part by a surgical instrument.
-tron	(specified) type of vacuum tube.
trop-	turn, turning, tendency, affinity.
-tropal	turn or change in the visual axis.
-trope	influence, influenced by.
troph-	food, nourishment.
-troph	that which nourishes an embryo.
-trophic	a specified type of nutrition; specified nutritional requirement.
-trophic	a type of nutrition, nutritional requirement.

T

tropho-	food, nourishment.
-trophy	condition of nutrition or growth.
-trophy	development, nourishment.
-trophy	development, nourishment.
-tropia	(condition of) deviation in the visual axis.
-tropia	(specified) deviation in the line of vision.
-tropia	to turn.
-tropic	turn or change in the visual axis.
-tropic	turning toward, having an affinity for.
-tropin	stimulating the function of (to turn or act on).
-tropism	having an affinity for something (specified).
tropo-	turn, turning, tendency, affinity.
-tropy	influenced by or having an affinity for something specified.
-tropy	tendency, tropism; turning reflecting.
-tumerscence	swelling.
-tuse	dull, blunt.

tympan-	eardrum, tympanic membrane.
-type	representative form, class.
typhlo-	cecum.
-typhoid	form of typus.
-typia	(condition of) conformity to type.
tyr-	cheese or cheese-like substance.
tyro-	cheese or cheese-like substance.
tyro-	cheese.

U

ul-	gums, gingival.
ul-	scar.
-ular	pertaining to something specified.
ulcero-	ulcer, ulcerous.
ule-	gums, gingival.
-ule	little, small.
ule-	scar.
-ulent	full of, characterized by.
uln-	ulna (lower arm bone.
ulo-	gums, gingival.
ulo-	scar, cicatrix.
ultra-	beyond, farther, beyond a certain limit.
-ulum	small one.
-ulus	small one.
-um	a combining form making singular nouns.
-um	structure, tissue.
umbilic-	navel, umbilicus.
un-	(prefix) not, without; to remove, deprive of.
ungu-	nail.

uni-	one.
ur-	caudal; tail, tail-like.
ur-	urine, urinary.
uran-	palate, palatal.
urano-	palate, palatal.
urano-	palate.
-urea	compound containing urea.
-uret	designating a binary compound.
ureter-	ureter.
urethra-	urethra.
urethro-	urethra.
-urgy	art of working with (specified) tools.
-uria	a (specified) condition of urine; the presence of a (specified) substance in urine.
-uria	presence of a substance in urine.
-uria	urine condition.
uric-	uric acid.
urico-	uric acid.
urico-	uric acid.
urin-	urine.
uro-	caudal; tail, tail-like.

U

uro-   urine, the urinary tract, urination.

uro-   urine, urinary.

urono-   urine, the urinary tract, urination.

-us   (suffix) designating an individual characterized by a (specified) trait or anomaly.

-us   a combining form signaling singular nouns.

-us   structure, substance.

uter-   uterus.

uve-   uvea; vascular layer of the eye (iris, ciliary body, and choroid).

uvula-   uvula.

-vaccine	preparation containing microorganizations for producing immunity to disease.
vag-	vagus nerve (10th cranial nerve).
vagin-	vagina.
vagino-	vagina.
vago-	vagus, vagal.
-valence	combining capacity of an atom compared with that of one hydrogen atom.
-valent	having a valency of a (specified) magnitude.
valv-	valve.
-valve	a thing that regulates the flow of.
valvul-	valve.
varic-	varicose veins.
varic-	vessel, duct; vas deferens.
vas-	vessel.
vascul-	vessel.
vaso-	vessel, duct.
ven-	vein.
veno-	vein.
-venous	of or referring to veins.

V

ventr-	front.
-ventral	of the stomach or abdominal region.
ventri-	belly, front side of the body.
ventricul-	ventricle, lower heart chamber.
ventriculo-	ventricle of the heart or brain.
ventro-	belly, front side of the body.
verd-	green-colored.
verdo-	green-colored.
vermi-	worm.
-verse	to turn.
-version	act of turning.
-vert	person who has turned (metaphorically) in a specific direction.
vertebr-	vertebra(e), backbone(s).
-vertebral	spinal column.
vertebro-	vertebral column; vertebra.
vesic-	urinary bladder.
vesico-	bladder, blister
vestibule-	vestibule.
viscer-	internal organs.
viscero-	organs of the body.

visuo-	vision, visual.
vit-	life.
vita-	life.
vitr	glass.
vitre-	glossy.
viv	life.
vivi-	alive, living.
-volemia	(condition of the) volume of plasma in the body.
-volute	to roll, turn around.
-vorous	eating, feeding on.
-vorous	referring to feeding on something specified.
vulva-	vulva.

X

xantho-	yellow.
xen-	different, foreign; alien, intrusive.
xeno-	strange, foreign matter.
xenous-	host.
xer	dry.
xero-	dryness.
xiph-	xiphid.
xiphi-	sword, xiphoid process.
xiphi-	xiphoid.
xipho-	sword, xiphoid process.
xipho-	xiphoid.
Xyl-	wood.
xylo-	wood.

Y

-y   condition, process.

-y   process, condition.

-yl   a univalent chemical radical; a radical contqining oxygen.

-yne   (suffix) denoting an unsaturated straight-chain hydrocarbon having one triple bond.

Z

z	impedance
zo-	animal life.
zo(o)	animal.
-zoic	a (specified) mode of animal life.
-zoite	simple organism.
zoo-	animal.
-zoon	living being.
zyg-	union, fusion, yoked, joined, a junction.
zyg-	yoke, joining; union, fusion; pair.
zygo-	union, fusion, yoked, joined, a junction.
-zygosity	relationship to the zygote
zym-	denoting fermentation, ferment; enzyme.
-zyme	ferment, enzyme.
zymo-	denoting fermentation, ferment; enzyme.
-zonular	pertaining to a small zone; as of a zone.
zoo-	animal; animal kingdom

CREDITS

B. A. Reed, Contributing Editor

B.A. Reed, contributing Editor, and Director of American Commercial College, San Angelo, Texas, began his career in vocational and technical education in 1974 as the campus director of a career school. During the last 35 years, he has served on many City, State, and Federal advisory and regulatory boards. He is the only individual in the State of Texas who has served on the Career Colleges and Schools Association Board in each of four separate decades serving as Board Chairman in 1996. His focus has been developing effective teaching approaches that unleash application learning that produces skills and performance.

Mr. Reed believes that specialized career education is the quickest and most effective vehicle for a person to enter the professional workforce and reach their God intended potential. Post-secondary education is the necessary preparatory foundation to the life-long learning experience that starts on the job.

Eva M. Brown-Beene, Research & Development Editor

Appreciation is expressed to Eva M. Brown-Beene, Anatomy & Physiology Instructor, San Angelo, Texas, whose work in research and development provided a valuable resource toward the compilation of this work.

Eva M. Brown-Beene, Editor, formerly Eva M. Brown-Burkett, is author of "Angels are Celestial Spirits", and forthcoming, "The Employ of Angels". She is co-author of forthcoming "Forever a Cowboy". She has also copyrighted "A&P-Opoly" a board game used in her Anatomy & Physiology classroom.

Cover design by Olga Verastegui

Olga Verastegui is an instructor at American Commercial College, San Angelo, Texas. She instructs students in Microsoft Programs, including: Access, Excel, PowerPoint, Outlook, Publisher and Word. Other works include GDP by Irving keyboarding. She received certification in Access and Excel by Microsoft.

RESEARCH CREDITS

Davi-Ellen Chabner. <u>The Language of Medicine.</u> Eight Edition

Mosby's. <u>Medical and Nursing Dictionary</u>

Blakiston's Gould Medical Dictionary. Third Edition

Ehrlich, Ann and Schroeder, Carol L. <u>Medical Terminology for Health Professions.</u> Fifth Edition

9 781438 966700